PRAISE FOR THIS BOOK

"Dr. Patrick Brill provides thorough and much-needed support for what many traditional-minded Catholics have long known or at least suspected: that St. Pius X's 1903 motu proprio *Tra le Sollectitudini* still provides the surest guide for the restoration of Catholic sacred music. Part I of this book provides a paragraph-by-paragraph commentary on the motu proprio, enlightening for amateur and expert alike, while Part II examines the fate of the document from the time of Pius to today, looking at its canonical force and status, positive efforts made to implement the reform, and the neglect it has suffered following Vatican II. Dr. Brill closes with a passionate yet reasonable plan for restoration. Throughout, he strikes an admirable balance: he neither talks over the head of the amateur nor talks down to the expert. Though he writes with fervor, he remains objective and almost entirely refrains from vitriol when speaking of the disastrous liturgical and cultural effects of Vatican II. As tradition continues to make crucial gains, it will be books like this that serve as practical guides for restoration. I am very happy to have it."

—**DR. ANDREW CHILDS**, B.Mus, DMA, former Associate Dean and Chair of Humanities at St. Mary's College; professional singer and choir conductor

"St. Pius X's 1903 motu proprio on sacred music is the bravest, loftiest, and most exhaustive attempt ever to protect and promulgate the precious musical riches of our Roman Rite. Its principles have never been fully realized, whether before or after the Council. Dr. Brill's work particularly shines by placing this great document in its tumultuous historic context and by thoroughly dismissing the naysayers who attempt to water down the urgency of this holy pope's directives."

—**JONATHAN BADING**, B.Mus., Director of Sacred Music, Sacred Heart of Jesus Catholic Parish, Grand Rapids, Michigan

"Patrick Brill's *The Great Sacred Music Reform of Pope St. Pius X* is an indispensable volume for every Catholic—musician or not—who wants to understand the sacred music of the Church.

Brill provides a detailed exegesis and history of Pius X's 1903 motu proprio on sacred music *Tra le Sollecitudini*, as well as the subsequent history of Catholic liturgical music through the aftermath of Vatican II. The author also offers a plan to help pastors and musicians restore sacred music in today's Catholic parishes, according to the evergreen reforms of St. Pius X."

—**SUSAN TREACY**, PhD, Professor of Music Emerita, Ave Maria University; author of *The Music of Christendom: A History*

"Despite the sorry state of music in the Church today, the official documents of the Church still clearly proclaim that Gregorian chant has 'first place' (*principum locum*) in the liturgy. Pope St. Pius X's motu proprio on sacred music is the definitive teaching on this subject. Brill's book is valuable for Church musicians, an immersion in the fundamentals. While some may take exception to certain interpretations of his, this book is a fascinating and important read."

—**FR. ROBERT C. PASLEY**, KCHS, Chaplain to the Church Music Association of America

"The musical reforms set in place by St. Pope Pius X were, perhaps, the most widespread such reforms since the flourishing of Gregorian chant in the Carolingian era. Even though they met with certain challenges in places, these reforms supported both the twentieth-century revival of chant and a renewed sensitivity to the importance of music in the liturgy. They were also summarily dismissed after Vatican Council II, since they were not compatible with the intended reforms to the Mass. Patrick Brill's study comes at an opportune moment, when Catholics are increasingly rejecting the banality of much of today's 'church music.' Brill's work conveniently gathers into a slim volume the historical context of Pius X's reforms, the reforms themselves, their implementation, and the place of these reforms in a Church rediscovering tradition. It will be a standard resource."

—**EDWARD SCHAEFER**, DMA, President of Collegium Sanctorum Angelorum; author of *Catholic Music Through the Ages*

THE GREAT SACRED MUSIC
REFORM OF POPE ST. PIUS X

OS JUSTI STUDIES IN CATHOLIC TRADITION

General Editor: Peter A. Kwasniewski

The Great Sacred Music Reform of Pope St. Pius X

*The Genesis, Interpretation,
and Implementation of the
Motu Proprio* Tra le Sollecitudini

PATRICK JOHN BRILL

OS JUSTI
PRESS

Os Justi Press
P.O. Box 21814
Lincoln, NE 68542
www.osjustipress.com

Send inquiries to
info@osjustipress.com

pbk 978-1-965303-10-8
hc 978-1-965303-11-5
ebook 978-1-965303-12-2

Layout by Michael Schrauzer
Cover by Julian Kwasniewski
Cover image:
Portrait of Pius X from *Die katholischen Missionen*,
October 1903, scanned by Stebunik; CC 3.0 license

A.M.D.G.

$\mathcal{C}$ontents

PREFACE TO NEW EDITION

THIS BOOK WAS INSPIRED BY TWO THINGS: first, the magnificent beauty of the great treasury of Catholic sacred music that has come down to us through the centuries; second, the realization of the full impact of the appalling neglect of this great treasury, particularly in the liturgy of the Roman Catholic Church, in the years following the Second Vatican Council.

Since the time of the Second Vatican Council (1962-1965), many Catholics and professional church musicians have been bewildered by the myriad senseless changes in the music and liturgy of the Roman Catholic Church. A comparison of the usual music in the new liturgy of the Mass, officially entitled the *Novus Ordo Missae*, with the music of the older Latin Tridentine Mass shows the unmistakable and extremely sharp contrasts between the two kinds of music, such that even those without the slightest musical education can readily tell the differences. This is because, simply put, the usual music of the *Novus Ordo* is shallow and fleeting, while that of the Tridentine Rite is profound and enduring (assuming that the music is performed correctly by competent musicians).

As time has passed, it has become painfully evident that there are (and have been for a long time) forces in the world, and even within the Catholic Church itself, that are determined to eradicate this musical treasury and to replace it with a style of "sacred music" that is not even deserving of the name. Many outstanding books have been written about these forces and their machinations, which books should be read by anyone who wants to know the deeper causes of this insidious debacle. Nevertheless, in spite of knowing the precise causes, the fact remains that the deleterious effects of these malevolent forces persist to this day.

On the other hand, there are also counter-forces in the Church today that are fighting to preserve this tradition; one sign of this is the return of the Latin Tridentine Mass in recent decades. This liturgical renaissance has taken the world by surprise as the number of Tridentine Masses has grown exponentially since the 1980s, especially during the fourteen years under Benedict XVI's *Summorum Pontificum*, with a following that includes large numbers of young people who are too young to have experienced the old rite in pre-Conciliar times. This last fact alone is enough to refute the fatuous argument that the restoration of the Tridentine Mass is due to some sort of liturgical "nostalgia." The truth is that these young Catholics perceive that the Tridentine Rite has something that the *Novus Ordo Missae* lacks, namely, the sense of the sacred, and a genuine sense of what is truly Catholic in the liturgy.

My project has two principal objectives: first, to assist Catholics dedicated to the restoration, preservation, and cultivation of sacred music in the Church today; second, to give those interested in the history of this treasury a solid foundation on which to build their knowledge, without the anti-Catholic bigotry and distortions so often found in contemporary academia, including nominally "Catholic" schools.

This book, on Pius X's motu proprio *Tra le Sollecitudini*, was developed out of a series of eight articles published in *Catholic Family News*, edited by Mr. John Vennari, in 2005. It is concerned with providing a detailed exposition of the thinking of Pope St. Pius X on the reform he initiated shortly after becoming pope in 1903. Pius's reform (endorsed and encouraged by other pre-Conciliar popes) developed, matured, and thrived through the years, lasting until the time of the Second Vatican Council. Having a clear understanding of its principles is crucial for a revival of the reform and the restoration of traditional Catholic sacred music; and there is no better way to have an understanding of the principles of the reform than to study the original document that launched that very reform.

Any renaissance of Western classical music should include a restoration of Catholic sacred music, since it is the latter that gave birth to the former in the first place. Thus, those who are interested in preserving and fostering Western classical music will find much in this project that will be of value to their objectives.

Finally, in connection with this project, I would like to acknowledge the kind support and encouragement of the late Mr. John Vennari and Dr. John Kaess, Br. Gregory Rice SSPX, Dr. Peter Kwasniewski, and last but by no means least, my wife, Fang Cecilia Brill.

Patrick John Brill
November 22, 2024
Feast of St. Cecilia

PART I

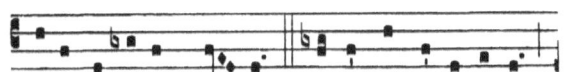

Principles of
the Reform

CHAPTER 1
The Principles

NOVEMBER 22, 1903, THE FEAST OF ST. Cecilia, saw the promulgation of one of the greatest pieces of papal legislation on sacred music in the history of the Church: Pope St. Pius X's motu proprio *Tra le Sollecitudini*.[1] This legislation inaugurated a long-awaited reform of sacred music that had been in preparation for many years. In this one document, Pius X accomplishes three things: first, he summarizes the traditional principles of Catholic sacred music; second, he articulates the canonical foundation for the practice of sacred music;[2] and third, he launches a major reform of sacred music for the universal Catholic Church that would continue well beyond his own pontificate. By means of this document, Pope St. Pius X provides an important blueprint for the reform of sacred music—a reform that would last until the time of Vatican II.

As implied by the word "reform," all was not well with Catholic sacred music prior to 1903, as numerous abuses

---

[1] This motu proprio is best known by its original Italian title, *Tra le Sollecitudini*. (The Latin title is *"Inter Sollicitudines."*) The document is also referred to as the "motu proprio of 1903" to distinguish it from Pius X's other musical motu proprio, *Col nostro* of 1904, which promulgated the Vatican Edition of the Gregorian chant.

[2] Pius himself called his motu proprio of 1903 "the legal code of sacred music." See *Musicae Sacrae Disciplina* no. 3, as quoted in Robert Hayburn, *Papal Legislation on Sacred Music 95 AD to 1977 AD* (Collegeville, MN: Liturgical Press, 1979). Hereafter, Fr. Hayburn's text will be referred to as "PLSM."

had been occurring throughout the nineteenth century in various parts of the world, including many churches in Italy. These abuses may come as a surprise to traditional Catholics who have witnessed, over the past sixty years, the utter destruction of virtually all aspects of their religion by neo-Modernists. Many readers will remember the halcyon days before Vatican II, before the reign of desecration that began when Archbishop Bugnini and his liturgical wrecking crews rampaged through our churches like wild bulls in a china shop, leaving everything in shambles. Many will also remember how, in the wake of Vatican II, traditional sacred music was abruptly withdrawn from the liturgy and replaced by cheap, vulgar, tawdry, and thoroughly secularized music. This abomination was foisted on congregations by local Ordinaries with the help of untrained "musicians" who knew, at best, three or four chords on the guitar, and who could barely sing in tune. Therefore, some readers may be justifiably puzzled that there were abuses in sacred music as early as 1903.

But abuses there were. In the Introduction of the motu proprio of 1903, Pope St. Pius X articulates the central problem of the reform:

> We do not propose to touch on all the abuses that may occur in these matters. We devote Our attention today to one of the commonest of abuses, one of the most difficult to uproot, and one that We sometimes have to regret, even in places where everything else, the beauty and splendor of the building, the dignity and accurate order of the ceremonies, the number of the clergy who attend, the gravity and piety of the celebrant, deserve the highest praise. We speak of abuses in the matter of the singing and of sacred music. And indeed, whether as a result of the changeable nature of this art, or of the many alterations in people's taste and custom during the lapse of time;

whether from the unhappy influence of secular
and theatrical music on that of the Church, or
from the pleasure excited by the music itself,
which it may not be easy to retain within proper
limits; whether, lastly, it be because of the many
prejudices on this subject which sometimes obsti-
nately remain, even among persons of great piety
and high authority, there certainly is a constant
tendency in sacred music to neglect the right
principles of an art used in the service of the liturgy, principles expressed very clearly in the laws
of the Church, in the decrees of general and pro-
vincial councils, and in the repeated commands
of the sacred congregations and of the supreme
pontiffs, Our predecessors.[3]

These abuses, as we will see in more detail, consisted
of such things as texts of the Mass set to operatic music,
improperly trained musicians, poor musical execution of
many singers, the use of prohibited instruments during
the liturgy, and many other problems. It is also interesting to note that Pius lauded the many churches where all
other aspects of the liturgy were practiced in a praisewor-
thy manner. Yet for various reasons there was (and still
is) "a constant tendency to neglect the right principles
of an art used in the service of the liturgy..." Today, of
course, the situation is far worse in contemporary *Novus
Ordo* churches where there is (and has been since Vatican
II) a constant tendency to neglect the right principles of
anything liturgical.

HISTORICAL BACKGROUND

Before proceeding to the principles of the motu proprio, it is important to examine its historical background.
This background provides the proper historical context in
which to interpret and understand the document.

---

[3] PLSM 222–23.

The motu proprio of 1903 was intended for the whole church. Nevertheless, even though it contained many clear and straightforward passages, it was directed, primarily, at *professional* Catholic Church musicians, as well as cardinals and local Ordinaries charged with its implementation and enforcement. Among professional musicians, these included, *inter alia*, the leaders of Catholic Church music in the world, such as choir directors, music professors, music journal writers, important composers, performers, directors of learned musical organizations, religious orders, and directors of Catholic music societies.[4]

These musicians possessed an extensive knowledge of the technical details of sacred music, including such subjects as harmony, form, counterpoint, orchestration, and composition. Most would have been highly proficient performers on one or more musical instruments, particularly the organ; if they were music directors of a parish or cathedral, they would have been competent in choral and orchestral conducting as well, and not a few were themselves composers. Many would be conversant in Western music history from the medieval period to 1903. Moreover, all would have known quite thoroughly, of course, the liturgies of the Mass and the Divine Office. It follows from these facts that Pius presupposed a considerable background of musical knowledge for a full understanding of his legislation.

Another important historical aspect concerns Giuseppe Sarto's own musical background, and his attitude toward Catholic sacred music. Anyone who has read a competent

---

[4] Numerous documents confirm the statements in this paragraph, including those issued by Pius X, Benedict XV, Pius XI, and Pius XII, as well as letters written by curial cardinals and documents from the Sacred Congregation of Rites. In addition, a cursory look at the implementation of Church institutions devoted to sacred music by Pius X alone would more than substantiate this paragraph. We will examine several of these documents later in this book.

biography of Pope St. Pius X will know that this holy pope greatly revered sacred music; that he possessed considerable knowledge of music in general; that he had some superb musical training as a young man under one Fr. Jacuzzi, a learned musician and priest from Pius's home parish; and that as early as his first parish assignment as an assistant pastor, the young Fr. Sarto was busy forming various *scholae* and avidly promoting the traditional music of the Church. He was also an ardent admirer of the Solesmes monks, who had recently achieved their monumental restoration of Gregorian chant. Most significantly, it was during these years that Fr. Sarto realized the extent of the musical abuses plaguing the Catholic Church.[5]

As Fr. Sarto progressed through the ecclesiastical ranks, he not only continued to promote the Church's traditional sacred music, he became a formidable enemy of those who abused their sacred privileges as church musicians. His chief weapon in eradicating these abuses was ecclesiastical legislation. Thus, when he became bishop of Mantua, Bishop Sarto enacted significant laws to combat the abuses he had found in his own diocese.

The *Synodal Decrees* of 1888 are an important set of documents from his tenure at Mantua that contain legislation on sacred music. Overall, the *Synodal Decrees* address mostly non-musical subjects; however, sections 25, 30, and 31 consider some major issues on sacred music occurring at the time. For example, Bishop Sarto commands that seminarians be thoroughly trained in Gregorian chant; that "bands" be prohibited from playing in church; that the only non-vocal instrument in the liturgy be the organ (except for special occasions when some instruments besides the organ could be used); and that Gregorian chant be given priority in the liturgy.

---

[5] PLSM 195–97.

When Bishop Sarto was elevated to Cardinal-Patriarch of Venice, he continued to promote sacred music. Two of the most important documents from this time are the *Votum* of 1893 and the *Pastoral Letter* of 1895. The *Votum* has some of the greatest writing on the philosophy of Catholic sacred music ever issued, while the *Pastoral Letter* contains, among other things, stiff canonical penalties for infringing the rules of sacred music. It also reinforces the basic principles articulated in the *Votum*. The *Votum* is in many ways the true foundation document for both the *Pastoral Letter* and the motu proprio of 1903. It is thus worth examining very briefly.

The *Votum* is divided into three parts: "General Considerations," "Particular Observations," and the "Instruction on Sacred Music." The first part is, in my opinion, one of the finest expositions of Catholic sacred music ever written. Fr. Hayburn remarks that this part "was a study of the principles which regulate sacred music and a refutation of the arguments presented by those who opposed the reform of Church music."[6] In addition to Fr. Hayburn's observations, this section actually amounts to a most enlightening formal exposition of the philosophy of Catholic sacred music. The second part is a history of the reform movement in Europe. In this section, Cardinal Sarto takes special aim at the abuse of bringing theatrical (i.e., operatic style) music into the Church. The third part is also important for understanding the motu proprio because, with the exception of a few sentences, the paragraphs in this part of the *Votum* are almost identical to the second part of the motu proprio, which is also entitled: "Instruction on Sacred Music." It is no exaggeration, then, to state that this motu proprio is simply the third part of the *Votum* of 1893 with a new introduction.

---

[6] PLSM 204.

It is also difficult to imagine fully comprehending the motu proprio without having read the *Votum*.

The *Pastoral Letter* of 1895 begins with an introduction that considers the true purposes of Catholic sacred music. It then threatens severe penalties for using any profane (i.e., secular) music in the liturgy, and, *inter alia*, it mandates the establishment of a *Schola Cantorum* in every parish in Venice for singing Gregorian chant. Because they shed such important light on the motu proprio, these documents will be referred to again throughout this book.

One last historical aspect that should be mentioned is that Pius's great reform would require a strong institutional Church for its implementation. In 1903, unlike today, the institutional Catholic Church was like a great hierarchical pyramid with the pope at the top, below which the cardinals, bishops, priests, and laity formed the rest of the pyramid. The cement holding the structure together was true obedience grounded on a lively orthodox Faith. Pius used this pyramid, and every one of its relevant institutions, to implement his reforms, including curial congregations, seminaries, parishes, dioceses, religious institutes, pontifical music schools, Catholic colleges and universities, as well as a whole array of commissions to oversee the implementation and enforcement of the reform. Pius was relentless in his assault on sacred music abuses. Without this strong institutional structure, his reform would probably never have succeeded.

Today, however, with the current problems plaguing the institutional Church, a reform of this magnitude would probably not succeed.[7] Later in this book, more will be said about what traditionalists can do to reform

---

[7] See Romano Amerio, *Iota Unum: A Study of the Changes in the Catholic Church in the XXth Century*, trans. Fr. John P. Parsons (Kansas City, MO: Sarto House, 1996).

sacred music in the midst of the terrible crisis within the contemporary Roman Catholic Church.

When Giuseppe Cardinal Sarto was elevated to the throne of Peter on August 9, 1903, he took the name of Pius X and chose as his motto: "To restore all things in Christ." He immediately began doing just that. One of the first things he set out to accomplish was the reform of sacred music for the *entire* Church. In case anyone might think that Pius was not serious about his reform, let him read the terse words of Bishop Casartelli: "His Holiness is credited with an intention to prosecute with vigor, at no distant date, the much needed reform of sacred music. This will be a day for which many, both clergy and laity, have long been anxiously looking."[8]

On November 22, 1903, just three and a half months after being elevated to the papacy, Pope Pius X promulgated his motu proprio.

THE TWO PRINCIPAL PARTS OF THE MOTU PROPRIO OF 1903

The motu proprio of 1903 is composed of two principal parts: an "Introduction" and an "Instruction on Sacred Music." The "Introduction" includes the articulation of the problem and the reasons for the reform, as well as a paragraph that formally binds the entire Church to the laws contained in the document. The "Instruction on Sacred Music" is an exposition of the principles of sacred music. It is divided into nine subdivisions each with its own title: I. General Principles, II. Various Kinds of Sacred Music, III. The Liturgical Text, IV. The External Form of Sacred Music, V. The Singers, VI. The Organ and Other Instruments, VII. The Length of Liturgical Music, VIII. The Chief Means of Procuring Good Sacred Music, IX. Conclusions.

---

[8] PLSM 219.

INTRODUCTION OF THE MOTU PROPRIO OF 1903

Regarding the "Introduction," we saw earlier that Pius X began his prosecution of the reform due to the many abuses he had found in sacred music. Now given that the new pope was faced with many urgent difficulties, including the gathering storm in European politics, as well as the extremely grave problem of Modernism and its baleful influence on the Church, why was Pius, as pope of the Church, so preoccupied with sacred music reform that it became a veritable top priority of his papacy? The answer to this question is presented at the very outset of the "Introduction" to the motu proprio:

> One of the chief duties of the pastoral office, not only in this Holy See which We, although unworthy, by the inscrutable decree of Providence occupy, but in every diocese of the Church, is certainly to maintain and increase the beauty of the house of God, in which the holy mysteries of our faith are celebrated, in which the Christian people come together to receive the grace of the Sacraments, and to assist at the Holy Sacrifice of the Altar, to adore the Blessed Sacrament, and to join in the public and solemn liturgical prayers of the Church. Nothing then should be allowed in the sacred building that could disturb or lessen the piety and devotion of the faithful, nothing that could be a reasonable motive for displeasure or scandal, nothing especially that could offend against the dignity and holiness of the sacred rites, and that would therefore be unworthy of the house of prayer, or of the majesty of Almighty God.[9]

Indeed, maintaining and increasing the beauty of the house of God truly is "one of the chief duties of the pastoral office." Thus, Pius was not about to let *anything*

---

[9] Motu proprio of 1903 as quoted in PLSM 222.

profane the house of God, including inappropriate music. Clearly, he was extremely diligent in fulfilling the duties of his office. This, of course, is in stark contrast to more recent popes, who have seriously neglected their pastoral office on this and other scores. Objectively speaking, for post-Conciliar popes to promote, or even allow, the current liturgical disorder to occur in so many Catholic churches throughout the world for sixty years is obviously a form of negligence in that high office.

In order to emphasize the degree of righteous indignation that Pius held for not only bad sacred music, but also *badly performed* sacred music, ponder this quotation from the *Pastoral Letter* of 1895, which was promulgated when he was Cardinal-Patriarch of Venice:

> You are aware how external cult contributes to stimulate piety and devotion; and among the actions of cult a most powerful part is played by the chant, which according to St. Bernard "in the Church makes glad the minds of men, gives delight to the blasé, prods on the sluggish, brings sinners to contrition; for no matter how hard may be the hearts of worldlings, they are drawn together to a love of devotion once they have heard the sweetness of the Psalms." But, if we are to have these salutary effects, it is necessary that the chant be as the Church prescribes. Otherwise, just as the profane ornaments of the drawing-room are unbecoming the majesty of the temple, so, too, and in a much greater degree, is triviality in chant or music. By reasons of this we might well provoke the chastisement inflicted on Aaron, Nadab, and Abiu, who, for using profane fire for the sacrifice, were consumed by a fire sent from heaven: "And fire coming from the Lord destroyed them, and they died before the Lord." This chastisement we might also provoke by reason of the scandal

which such profane music gives, not only to the
good, who are distracted by it in their devotions,
but to the heterodox and schismatics, whom I
myself have often heard deplore such profana-
tions, and thus "In us Christ shares our shame,
and the Christian law our curse . . ." O venera-
ble priests, let us not make ourselves guilty of
this great sacrilege . . . [10]

When Pius laments what he calls "triviality in chant
or music," he is referring first to improperly rendered
chant, i.e., Gregorian chant that is sung either by poorly
trained singers who make constant and unforgivable
mistakes, or by singers who interpret the music in a
secular way. Second, regarding polyphonic music, he is
pointing to the illicit use of secular compositions in the
liturgy, which in itself — no matter how well they are
performed — is, along with poorly rendered chant, an
egregiously sacrilegious profanation of the liturgy. To Pius,
all of these abuses come dangerously close to provoking
the just wrath of the Lord God Himself, similar to the
wrath in which God "drove out of the temple those who
were profaning it."[11] Thus, Pius likens the abusers of
sacred music to the moneychangers (and others), who
so profaned the Temple of Jerusalem at the time of Jesus.

If the reader has any lingering doubts concerning this
pope's meaning and determination, let the final paragraph of the "Introduction" of the motu proprio, in which
he binds the whole Church to his legislation, signal the

---

[10] *Pastoral Letter* of 1895 as quoted in PLSM 218. I wish the reader
to understand that I am not making any kind of judgment regarding the internal act, or the eternal destiny, of any post-Conciliar
pope. Rather, for this current crisis to have continued this long is
a serious indication of *objective negligence*, or at the very least, a
serious problem in the Vatican caused by hostile forces interfering
with the pope's agenda.

[11] Motu proprio of 1903, as quoted in PLSM 223.

firm intent of this pontiff to eradicate thoroughly all sacred music abuses:

> Wherefore, in order that no one may in the future put forward as an excuse that he does not rightly know his duty, in order that all possible uncertainty concerning laws already made may be removed, We consider it advisable to sum up shortly the principles that govern the sacred music of liturgical services, and to present again the chief laws of the Church against faults in this matter. And therefore We publish this Our Instruction *motu proprio et ex certa scientia* ["on our own accord and from certain knowledge"], and We desire with all the authority of Our apostolic office that it have the force of law as a canonical code concerning sacred music, and We impose upon all by Our own signature the duty of the most exact obedience to it. [12]

Indeed, this paragraph leads directly to a summation of the "principles that govern the sacred music of liturgical services." This sentence is alluding to the next section entitled: "Instruction on Sacred Music," in which the context is strictly sacred music in *liturgical services.* The last part of this paragraph indicates that Pius is using *all* of his authority as supreme pontiff of the Catholic Church to make his legislation "have the force of law as a canonical code concerning sacred music." This means that he is imposing a set of canonical precepts on "*all,*" i.e., everyone in the Church. He is clearly commanding, with all of the jurisdictional authority Jesus Christ has invested in him, *strict* obedience to every one of his precepts.

---

[12] PLSM 223. Obviously, Pius X will still allow those using other approved rites of the Catholic Church to continue their use of those rites; this at any rate is not something that would be in his competence to disallow.

CHAPTER 2
The "Instruction on Sacred Music"

GENERAL PRINCIPLES

The "Instruction on Sacred Music" begins with an exposition of the general principles of sacred music. These principles include two aspects: first, the goals of Catholic sacred music, and second, the qualities that are proper to liturgical music.

Pius commences the "Instruction" by articulating the purposes of sacred music:

> 1. Sacred music, being an integral part of the liturgy, is directed to the general object of this liturgy, namely, the glory of God and the sanctification and edification of the faithful. It helps to increase the beauty and splendor of the ceremonies of the Church, and since its chief duty is to clothe the liturgical text, which is presented to the understanding of the faithful, with suitable melody, its object is to make that text more efficacious, so that the faithful through this means may be the more roused to devotion, and better disposed to gather to themselves the fruits of grace which come from the celebration of the sacred mysteries.[1]

Here St. Pius introduces us to the hierarchy of goals for Catholic sacred music, which music forms a *pars*

[1] PLSM 223-224. Regarding the Mass, it should be remembered that the principal context of the motu proprio of 1903 is the sung liturgy, i.e., a Missa Cantata (High Mass) or a *Missa Solemnis*.

integrans of the liturgy. The first goal, which is the remote goal of sacred music, is the honor and glory of God. Music shares this purpose, and thus nobility, with all other aspects of the liturgy, including the other fine arts used in the liturgy. There can be no loftier purpose for an art than to render honor and glory to God.

Beyond this goal are several proximate ends for sacred music. For St. Pius states that music "helps to increase the beauty and splendor of the ceremonies of the Church." This is because its primary duty is to "clothe the liturgical text" for the understanding of the faithful with "suitable melody." Thus, melody makes the text more attractive so the faithful will be inspired to greater devotion. In addition, since music is the only art that can adorn a text with "suitable melody," the composer will be able to use all of the available emotional subtleties of music to adorn the text, and thus inspire greater devotion.

However, this greater devotion becomes a means to another end, which is to assist the congregation in gathering more fruits of the graces that come from the "celebration of the sacred mysteries." At Mass, for example, graces flow from the sacrament when a validly ordained Catholic priest, using valid matter and form (as well as the proper intention), consecrates the bread and wine, turning them into the Body and Blood of Jesus Christ. When the sacrament is thus validly consecrated, graces pour forth in abundance. Moreover, with its many other graces, the Mass provides a great wealth of graces to the devout faithful.

Now even though there are abundant graces, not everyone is necessarily equally disposed to the *reception* of these graces. Those who are better disposed will receive more graces than those not as well disposed. Music, then, plays a most crucial role in assisting the faithful to receive more of the graces flowing from the sacraments of the sacred liturgy. The more graces we have, the better we are able to live Christian lives here on earth, and the greater will be our reward in heaven. It is thus evident why Pope St. Pius X gives the sacred music of the Church such high priority—and why we should as well.

> 2. Sacred music must therefore eminently possess the qualities which belong to the liturgical rites, especially holiness and beauty, from which its other characteristic, universality, will follow spontaneously.
>
> It must be holy, and therefore avoid everything that is secular, both in itself and in the way in which it is performed.
>
> It must really be an art, since in no other way can it have on the mind of those who hear it that effect which the Church desires in using in her liturgy the art of sound.
>
> But it must also be universal in this sense, namely, that although each country may use in its ecclesiastical music whatever special forms may belong to its own national style, these forms must be subject to the proper nature of sacred music, so that it may never produce a bad impression on the mind of any stranger who may hear it. [2]

The first paragraph of no. 2 presents the three qualities of the liturgy which sacred music must possess: holiness, art, and universality. By holiness, Pius means that liturgical music must be thoroughly imbued with the *sensus sacrae*, from which it follows that it will be devoid of the secular. It must have the sense of the sacred both *in itself* and in the way it is *performed*. This last distinction is not merely academic. When Pius writes that a composition must possess the sense of the sacred "in itself," he

---

[2] PLSM 224.

means that the composition, considering only the tonal relationships themselves, must be free of all traces of the secular. By "secular," Pius includes theatrical, sentimental, and "popular" styles, indeed, any music that suggests or connotes, in any way, the secular.

Pius also condemns, equally, the *performance* of a legitimate sacred composition that would suggest or connote the secular. To understand this, it is crucial to make some distinctions, and refute a common misconception.

Remember that music, of its very nature, is a performing art, as opposed to a "static" fine art, such as painting, sculpture, or architecture, in which the artist is the sole originator of the material object. A performing art is one in which time, movement, and intermediary creative interpreters are required to execute a piece. For just as dance makes use of exterior bodily movements through time *by means of a creative interpreter of dance*, so also music, the art of sound, makes use of the movement of sounds through time *by means of a creative musical interpreter*. Therefore, all music must be performed. Since Catholic sacred music is music, therefore, all Catholic sacred music must be performed; thus, viewed from an efficient causal context, it is a species of performing art. Now, since all music is a type of performing art, it must be interpreted by a competent performer capable of rendering a good artistic interpretation. An incompetent performer distorts a composition by rendering a poor interpretation. (This situation can happen in *any* performing art, be it theater, dance, mime, or music.) A good performer, of course, will render a good interpretation. However, when a performer deliberately gives secular connotations to a performance of a Catholic sacred music composition that has been composed thoroughly with the *sensus sacrae*, or when that performer is simply an incompetent performer, he or she effectively destroys the purity of the *sensus sacrae*. This is what Pius is condemning here, along with the use of purely secular compositions. Thus, all Catholic sacred liturgical music must possess thoroughly and completely the sense of the sacred, both in itself and in the way it is performed.

At this point, it is appropriate to dispel a common misconception concerning the word "performance." Some Catholics condemn the use of professional-sounding choirs in the liturgy because the liturgy, in their view, then becomes a "performance" in the sense of a concert in which people come to church only to listen to, and be entertained by, well-performed music.

The response to this fallacious argument is that Pius is only using the word "performance" in the sense of music being "executed" or "rendered." Thus, describing music as being "well performed" is for Pius the same as saying that the music is "well executed" or "well rendered." Now what turns a liturgy into a secular "public concert" is precisely music that contains *secular* elements, whether *in itself* or in the way it is *performed*! Moreover, when this secular music is well performed, it is even worse because it makes that which is *profane* more attractive; on the other hand, if true sacred music is well performed, it makes that which is *sacred* far more beautiful.

Pius also proscribes the use of Catholic sacred music if it is *poorly performed*. This issue goes well beyond the problem of an interpretation that connotes the secular. Rather, it bears on the question of the competence and skill of the choir itself. Even a cursory examination of the kind of musical training that Pius X demanded of church musicians in his reform will amply demonstrate that for him, sacred music must not be left to rank amateurs. Rather, as Pius admonishes, choirs should be comprised of properly *trained* musicians, i.e., those having the requisite musical skills to give a correct rendition, such as voice training, sight-reading skills, aural skills, and an adequate knowledge of the repertoire. This does not mean that everyone in the choir must be a graduate of Juilliard or the Paris Conservatory. Nor is it a requirement that one be a famous solo performer, such as Luciano Pavarotti. Nevertheless, all choir members should have had competent, professional training at the level of a standard college music curriculum, or equivalent private training from qualified music instructors. As we will see, Pius even insists upon the establishment of diocesan commissions to oversee the quality of musicianship and sacred music in their respective dioceses.

These standards also apply to choral directors, who should possess correct vocal training and must be competent in such subjects as conducting, repertoire, liturgy, music history, music theory, and preferably, musical composition. Directors must know how to maintain in their choirs proper "blend," correct intonation, diction, tempo, and rhythm, to name just a few. They must also impart a correct interpretation that is free of all secular connotations, thus bringing about a pure sense of the sacred. Without these skills, directors will be seriously handicapped in their ability to render correctly a sacred musical composition. (Later, we will examine some of the documents that show the extent and complexity of Pius's musical curricula at various academic levels in Church-sponsored schools.)

Pius insisted on these standards because he knew that only a well-trained choir under the direction of a well-trained music director, who has chosen only genuine Catholic sacred music, and whose interpretation faithfully renders the *sensus sacrae* in a musically correct manner, would achieve truly Catholic standards in music.

For Pius X, anything less than these musical standards constituted liturgical abuse.

Now if the reader believes that this is unduly critical of untrained choirs, let me quote Cardinal Sarto's own words as found in the *Pastoral Letter* of 1895. Please remember that passages similar to the following one occur in many places in the writings of Pius X, in documents on sacred music by Pius X's successors, as well as in communications from the Congregation of Sacred Rites:

> 14. The Sacred Congregation of Rites justly notes that a composition, even though in itself excellent polyphonic music, may become unsuitable by *bad execution*; it therefore firmly prescribes that where good music is lacking *or cannot be rendered fittingly*, it shall be obligatory to use the Gregorian chant in strictly liturgical functions. [3]

When Pius remarks "it shall be obligatory to use the Gregorian chant in strictly liturgical functions," the context here is a choir that is competent to sing the chant, but not able to render a more complex polyphonic composition correctly. Let it be noted, however, that if a choir were to make even the Gregorian chant "unsuitable by bad execution," Pius would make it obligatory for that choir to be *silent*.

The third paragraph of no. 2 articulates the *second* quality of sacred music:

> It must really be an art, since in no other way can it have on the mind of those who hear it that effect which the Church desires in using in her liturgy the art of sound. [4]

Here Pius X introduces the essential concept of sacred music as *art*. Pius's concept of "art" can be more clearly

---

[3] *Pastoral Letter* of 1895 as quoted in PLSM 218; emphasis added.
[4] Motu proprio of 1903 as quoted in PLSM 224.

expressed and understood by English technical phrases such as "integrity of form" or "excellence of form."

The term "integrity of form" means the musical relations in a composition in which the various musical parameters, such as melody, harmony, rhythm, meter, tempo, and the like, all work together in a systematic order to produce the emotional effects of the whole. To understand this concept in depth, of course, requires an extensive technical knowledge of musical composition. However, an analogy to the theater will help with an initial understanding of Pius's meaning.

Integrity of form in music is similar to a play in which the plot is connected logically by the sequence of events having a cause-and-effect relationship. Thus, one event sets up the next, and is a logical outcome of the preceding actions, particularly when the characters act according to their mode of characterization. The integrity of the play is also considerably enhanced when the scenery, lighting, costumes, acting, and the like are related to the specific events of the plot. Thus, in a play that has integrity of form, *all* elements contribute to the effect of the whole in a logical way, which then conveys the actions and resulting emotions of the play in a most effective way.[5]

Similarly, music consists of complex tonal relationships in which the sequence of emotions follows a kind of "musical-logical" order. Various emotions are presented to create an overall emotional effect. Each passage expresses an emotion related to the next passage by musical means such as, for example, motivic units, which are small musical fragments that bind the various passages together, thus creating musical continuity in the sequence of emotions. Each musical parameter works

---

[5] See Aristotle's *Poetics*, in *Aristotle's Theory of Poetry and Fine Art*, trans. S. H. Butcher (New York: Dover Publications, 1951).

together in a coherent manner to produce this sequence of emotions. In this way, for sacred music with integrity of form, the *sensus sacrae* will be most effectively presented to the congregation – an effectiveness it can have in no other way. In sacred music without integrity of form, the *sensus sacrae* will be considerably hindered, and thus ineffective. This is why Pius insists that sacred music must be art, "since in no other way can it have on the mind of those who hear it that effect which the Church desires in using in her liturgy the art of sound."

From these two qualities, holiness and art (i.e., the *sensus sacrae* and integrity of form), the third quality, universality, comes to be:

> But it must also be universal in this sense, namely, that although each country may use in its ecclesiastical music whatever special forms may belong to its own national style, these forms must be subject to the proper nature of sacred music, so that it may never produce a bad impression on the mind of any stranger who may hear it.[6]

Pius concludes that forms may be used which belong to the national style of a particular country, but that the other qualities of sacred music (integrity of form and the sense of the sacred) must still be present if it is to be true sacred music. Thus, Pius provides the key which ensures that a sacred composition has universality; all composers need to do is make sure that the music has integrity of form and the *sensus sacrae*, from which universality will follow "spontaneously."

VARIOUS KINDS OF SACRED MUSIC

The next section addresses the three kinds of music for use in the Catholic liturgy: Gregorian chant, classical

---

6 Motu proprio of 1903 as quoted in PLSM 224.

polyphony, and modern sacred music. Pius begins with the *first* kind of music, Gregorian chant:

> 3. These qualities [i.e., holiness, art, and universality] are found most perfectly in Gregorian chant, which is therefore the proper chant of the Roman Church, the only chant which she has inherited from the ancient Fathers, which she has jealously kept for so many centuries in her liturgical books, which she offers to the faithful as her own music, which she insists on being used exclusively in some parts of her liturgy, and which, lastly, has been so happily restored to its original perfection and purity by recent study.
>
> For these reasons Gregorian chant has always been looked upon as the highest model of Church music, and we may with good reason establish as a general rule that the more a musical composition for use in church is like Gregorian chant in its movement, its inspiration, and its feeling, so much the more is it right and liturgical, and the more it differs from this highest model so much the less is it worthy of the house of God.
>
> Wherefore, this ancient Gregorian chant should be largely restored in divine worship, and it should be understood that a service of the Church loses nothing of its solemnity when it is accompanied by no other music than Gregorian chant.
>
> Especially should this chant be restored to the use of the people, so that they may take a more active part in the offices, as they did in former times.[7]

In the first paragraph of no. 3, when Pius writes that the Church "insists on [chant] being used exclusively in some parts of her liturgy," he is referring mainly to those texts of a High Mass such as the Epistle, Gospel, Preface, the Lord's Prayer, and dialogues, which are never sung

---

[7] Ibid.

to anything but Gregorian chant. His mention of the restoration of chant refers, of course, to the great work of the Solesmes monks in France.[8]

The second paragraph indicates that chant is the highest exemplar of sacred music. Thus, the more a composition resembles the chant in its movement, style, and expression, the more worthy it is of the house of God. For the same reason, the more it differs from the chant, "so much the less is it worthy of the house of God." Now since he was not only a pope of words but also a pope of action, within just one year of the appearance of the motu proprio of 1903 Pius would issue the official Vatican Edition of Gregorian chant. This fruit of the long labors of the Solesmes monks was promulgated in the motu proprio *Col nostro* of 1904, which provided church musicians of the time with the best edition of Gregorian chant to be found anywhere in the world.

The third paragraph stresses that a liturgy comprised only of chant is just as solemn as a liturgy that has both chant and polyphony, or for that matter, has mostly polyphonic music in it. This is a rebuttal to the argument that the solemnity of a liturgy would be incomplete without at least some polyphonic music. Nevertheless, it does not mean that polyphony should only be used sparingly, or that there is a distinct preference for liturgies to have chant only.

In the fourth paragraph, Pius urges the use of chant for the *congregation* so that they may take "a more active part in the offices." This is referring not only to the Divine Office, but also to the chants of the Ordinary of the Mass: the Kyrie, Gloria, Credo, Sanctus/Benedictus, and Agnus Dei. It does not apply to the sung Propers of the Mass, such as the Introit, Gradual, Alleluia, Tract, Offertory,

---

[8] See *Paléographie musicale*, 17 vols., Solesmes, 1889–1925.

Communion, and the like. These Propers are the exclusive province of the choir; their level of difficulty alone makes this plain, as does their history of formation.

It is also important to note that Pius's stringent requirements for musical training do not apply to the congregation. Pius does not expect everyone in the pews to be a trained musician – although he certainly would not discourage anyone from taking vocal instruction. His condemnation of bad execution and secular interpretations is directed to singers, choirmasters, and celebrants.

Pius next turns to the *second* kind of music, namely, classical polyphony:

> 4. The qualities described above [i.e., holiness, art, and universality] are also found to a high degree in music of the classical school, especially in that of the Roman school, which reached its greatest perfection in the sixteenth century under Pierluigi da Palestrina, and which even afterwards went on producing excellent liturgical compositions.[9]

Pius begins with the statement that the three qualities of sacred music – holiness, art, and universality – that are so distinctive of Gregorian chant, are also found "to a high degree in the music of the classical school, especially in that of the Roman school, which reached its greatest perfection in the sixteenth century under Pierluigi da Palestrina." What are these "classical" and "Roman" schools? Moreover, who is Pierluigi da Palestrina?

By "classical school" Pius is referring to the repertoire of Catholic sacred polyphonic music composed chiefly by Catholic musicians employed by the Church, who flourished principally in the fifteenth and sixteenth centuries, mainly in what is today Italy, France, England, Spain, and Germany. Most of the genres in this repertoire are

---

[9] Motu proprio of 1903 as quoted in PLSM 225.

Masses and motets. Masses are polyphonic settings of the Ordinary of the Mass—typically (since the fourteenth century) the Kyrie, Gloria, Credo, Sanctus/Benedictus, and Agnus Dei. The other major genre of sacred music is the motet, which is a single movement polyphonic setting of any Church-approved text except those from the sung Ordinaries of the Mass. All of these compositions are characterized by a euphonious, linear, polyphonic style utilizing the same basic modal system as Gregorian chant, but with certain modifications in the modes to accommodate the exigencies of polyphony.

The classical school is a "school" in the sense of a common musical style that was consciously practiced by Catholic musicians throughout Europe and England.[10] It is not a school in the sense of a high school or college with classrooms, faculty, and an administration. Nevertheless, it should not be thought that there was no exchange of ideas, or private instruction. On the contrary, many of the great masters would periodically visit churches in Europe to observe the liturgy and exchange knowledge of the art and practice of sacred music. Many masters offered private lessons. Moreover, for members of a choir, instruction in the fundamentals of music would have been readily available to talented young musicians. In fact, in the fifteenth and sixteenth centuries, many musicians received their early musical instruction as child members of a church choir.

Now just as there are local dialects within various European languages, so also are there several regional musical

---

[10] Contemporary musicologists do not like the historical concept of compositional schools because it implies the use of universals. This is largely because most musicologists today have fallen into the error of Nominalism, which denies the existence of universals. Pius X, however, being a Thomist, and therefore a realist, acknowledges the existence of universals, and thus understands that there is nothing wrong epistemologically with the concept of compositional schools.

"dialects" of the classical sacred style. The word "dialect" is used here by analogy, since music is not a language in the strict sense of a real human language. Nevertheless, the parallel applies in that each musical "dialect," just like a linguistic dialect, has important similarities to the other dialects, as well as some distinctive features of its own.

In the middle and late sixteenth century there were several sub-styles (or "dialects") of classical polyphony located in various parts of Europe, such as the English school, the Spanish school, and the Roman school. All of these sub-styles had certain features in common with the general sacred style, which style was essentially the Flemish polyphony that had dominated sacred music since the early sixteenth century. Thus, when Pius writes of the "Roman school," he is referring to a distinct sub-style of Catholic polyphonic sacred music cultivated by Catholic composers working in various churches (mostly in Rome) in the middle and late sixteenth century. These church musicians worked closely with cardinals, bishops, and even popes in the development of sacred music, and thus knew the minds of ecclesiastical legislators.

As we will see shortly, polyphony has a long history dating back to the early Middle Ages. However, in the first half of the sixteenth century the Netherlands was the epicenter of development for classical polyphony. Flemish composers who worked in important churches in major European cities spread the style throughout the continent. Naturally, this influenced Rome itself, which employed many Flemish composers in key church positions. Gradually, as Italian composers adopted and then adapted the Flemish style, a local musical "dialect" was developed. Italian composers gradually took over many of these church posts and continued to cultivate the style, so that by the late sixteenth century the Roman had surpassed the Flemish in sophistication and profundity. The

Roman composer credited with refining this Roman style to its perfection is Pierluigi da Palestrina, the man Pius singles out as the greatest of the Roman school composers.

Giovanni Pierluigi da Palestrina was probably born *circa* 1525 in a small town outside of Rome known as Palestrina. He was trained in music from an early age in church choirs. His earliest instruction appears to have been at St. Maria Maggiore in Rome, where a document there lists a "Giovanni da Palestrina" among the choirboys. His teachers would have included the successive *maestri* (i.e., choirmasters) employed there at the time. These were the Frenchmen Robin Mallapert and Firmin Lebel, from whom he probably learned the Flemish style.

In his early professional career, around 1540, Palestrina held a choirmaster post at the Cathedral of Palestrina in the city of his birth. Later, he would become a *maestro* (at various times) at several of Rome's most prestigious churches and chapels, such as the Sistine Chapel, St. John Lateran, and St. Maria Maggiore. Moreover, during the years 1566–1571, he also taught music at the *Seminario Romano*.[11]

Palestrina composed one hundred and four settings of the Mass, and hundreds of motets and motet-like compositions, such as Magnificats, psalms, litanies, hymns, antiphons, and the like. He also composed both secular madrigals and spiritual madrigals; his fame, however, today rests principally on his sacred music output. It is this sacred output, of course, to which Pius is referring in the motu proprio of 1903.

Palestrina is also credited with "saving" sixteenth-century sacred polyphony from two Fathers of the Council of Trent (1545–1563). These Fathers desired to abolish

---

[11] Lewis Lockwood, *The New Grove High Renaissance Masters: Josquin, Palestrina, Lassus, Byrd, Victoria* (New York: Norton, 1984), 93–103.

all polyphonic music from the sacred liturgy. This legend has been somewhat exaggerated, but there is still some truth in it. Those Fathers who argued for the exclusive use of Gregorian chant in the liturgy were obviously misinformed about the importance of sacred polyphony. Fortunately, saner heads prevailed and easily overrode them. In fact, there is no substantial evidence that during the Council the idea of banning polyphony altogether ever went beyond the stage of a preliminary proposal.[12] At any rate, the better-informed Council Fathers, such as Cardinal Carlo Borromeo (known today as St. Charles Borromeo), and the *vast majority* of the Fathers of the Council of Trent, ordered classical polyphony to be reformed and retained.

Along historical lines, it is interesting to note that Pius scrupulously avoids modern musical-historical designations, such as "Renaissance," "Baroque," "Romantic," and the like. If one were to look up Palestrina's music in a music history textbook, he would find Palestrina's music classified as "Renaissance" music, with the dates of the musical Renaissance period being 1450 to 1600. This period is further subdivided into Early Renaissance: 1450–1500, "High" Renaissance: 1500–1550, and Late Renaissance: 1550–1600. According to this scheme, most of Palestrina's music would fall into the Late Renaissance. This designation, as well as its three sub-periods, is true and accurate to the extent that it applies to the *secular* music of the period. Indeed, the secular principles of the humanistic Renaissance do accord abundantly well with the secular music of the time. However, this designation becomes very misleading when applied to Catholic sacred music composed between 1450 and 1600. This is because (as we will see shortly) the development of classical polyphony precedes the historical

---

[12] Lockwood, 104–8.

Renaissance by about five centuries! Moreover, the word "Renaissance" as a period term was coined by secular historians. These historians would not necessarily have had an appreciation of the sense of the sacred, much less true sacred music. Thus, Pius omits these designations in order to avoid misleading and confusing terminology.

Earlier, we also saw that Pius stated that the Roman school reached its peak with Palestrina, "and . . . even afterwards went on producing excellent liturgical compositions." This passage is pointing to the fact that after Palestrina's death, Roman school composers continued to write compositions worthy of the liturgy of the Church. Examples of these composers are Tomás Luis de Victoria (1548 – 1611), the Anerio brothers – Giovanni (c. 1567 – 1630) and Felice (c. 1564 – 1614), Annibale Zoilo (1537 – 1592), the Nanino brothers – Giovanni Maria (c. 1543 – 1607) and Giovanni Bernardino (c. 1550 – 1623), Annibale Stabile (c. 1540 – c. 1595), Francesco Soriano (1549 – 1621), and many more. We should also remember that Pius is *not* excluding the Catholic liturgical music of other great classical polyphonic masters of the late sixteenth century, such as William Byrd (1543 – 1623), Orlando di Lasso (1532 – 1594), and Francisco Guerrero (1528 – 1599).[13]

Continuing with no. 4, Pius next articulates some important points vis-à-vis a comparison of Gregorian chant with that of classical polyphony:

---

[13] Tomás Luis de Victoria is sometimes classified as belonging to the "Spanish School." Although there is clear evidence of some Spanish style elements in his music, he nevertheless spent many years in Rome as both a student and choirmaster, and his music overwhelmingly shows the influence of the style of Palestrina, under whom he may have studied. See Patrick J. Brill, "Melody in the Motets of T. L. de Victoria and the Palestrina Style: A Comparative Analysis," M. M. Thesis, University of Northern Iowa, 1991. See also Walter D. Hirschl, "The Styles of Victoria and Palestrina: A Comparative Study, with Special References to Dissonance Treatment," M. A. Thesis, University of California, Berkeley, 1933.

> The music of the classical school agrees very
> well with the highest model of all sacred music,
> namely, Gregorian chant, and therefore it
> deserves, together with Gregorian chant, to be
> used in the more solemn offices of the Church, as,
> for instance, in those of the Papal Chapel. This
> music, too, should be largely restored, especially
> in the greater basilicas, in cathedrals, and in
> seminaries and other institutions where the nec-
> essary means of performing it are not wanting.[14]

When Pius writes that the music of the classical school
"agrees very well" with the chant, he means that classical
polyphony, too, possesses the three qualities of the liturgy – the *sensus sacrae*, integrity of form, and universality – "to a high degree." But does this make classical
polyphony equal to the chant? It appears that it does not,
because Pius writes in a passage quoted above that chant
is "the highest model of all sacred music." Yet classical
polyphony "agrees very well" with the chant insofar as
the three qualities of liturgy are concerned. Is not this
"agreement" the equivalent of saying that the two are
somehow equal? A passage from the *Votum* of 1893 sheds
some valuable light on this question:

> 4. The Church has known how to create and pro-
> pose to the world a twofold kind of music. This
> [twofold kind of music] corresponds fully and
> perfectly to the three qualities of sacred music
> which we mentioned above [i.e., holiness, art,
> and universality].
>
> b) . . . The classical polyphony, inspired by
> Gregorian chant, has in its form a character of
> sacredness and a mysticism so marked that the
> Church judged it fitting for the temple of God.
> In fact, it was so truly fitting as to stand side
> by side with Gregorian chant. It was because of

---

[14] Motu proprio of 1903 as quoted in PLSM 225.

this that it was employed in the most solemn
liturgical functions, such as those held in the
Pontifical Chapel.[15]

Now if classical polyphony corresponds "fully and perfectly" to the three requirements of sacred music, and if
this polyphony is so appropriate as to "stand side by side
with Gregorian chant," then is it not the equal of chant?
Should it not also be called, along with chant, one of "the
highest models of all sacred music?" One thing we can
conclude from this is that when Pius writes that polyphony "agrees very well" with the chant, he means that it
truly agrees "fully and perfectly" with the three qualities
of liturgical music. Thus, Pius is clearly implying that, at
least in this respect, they are indeed equal. Nevertheless,
if it is equal to the chant in this respect, why is it not
then "the highest model of all sacred music?" Why is
chant alone given what later church musicians will call
"pride of place?"

A partial answer to these questions is found by recall-
ing Pius's comments in the first paragraph of no. 3 in
the motu proprio, where he indicates that only Gregorian chant has been inherited from the ancient Fathers
of the Church, and thus has a long history dating back to
the early Church. He also mentions that only Gregorian
chant has been kept by the Church over the centuries in
her actual liturgical books, and is thus the only music
that the Church "offers to the faithful as her own music."
The argument is further bolstered by his comment that
there remain certain texts of the liturgy that can be sung
only in Gregorian chant – for example, the Epistle, Gospel,
and parts of the Canon in a High Mass. For these reasons,
therefore, chant is the highest model of all sacred music.

---

[15] Part I: General Considerations, *Votum* of 1893 as quoted in PLSM
206.

These answers point to certain deeper reasons why the chant has "pride of place" over classical polyphony, while at the same time polyphony corresponds "fully and perfectly" to the three requirements of sacred music. In order to obtain the kind of understanding of the relationship between Gregorian chant and classical polyphony needed to answer these questions in greater depth, it is imperative to examine briefly this historical development.

In the history of polyphony, Palestrina brings to a peak a polyphonic stylistic development that has its origins in the ninth century, possibly even earlier. Prior to this, there was no polyphony – no Western polyphonic music as we know it today. The only sacred music that existed was the monophonic Gregorian chant, alongside the various pagan musics of the Roman Empire and the "Barbarians," none of which was true Western polyphony or suitable for divine worship in the Church.

Now since liturgical chant probably existed as early as apostolic times, it preceded the classical polyphony by many centuries. The earliest chants seem to have consisted of simple syllabic and psalmodic melodies. Chants then underwent several centuries of development whereby this simple syllabic chant gave way to a neumatic style, and then to a more highly elaborate style known as melismatic.[16] This melismatic style reaches its peak about the tenth century. Chant composers proceeded to write in all styles, but emphasis was given to the more elaborate ones. As this development continued, composers even tried new techniques of elaboration such

---

[16] The term "syllabic" refers to a melody in which each syllable is set to a single note. "Neumatic" indicates the relationship of two to four notes of melody per syllable. "Melismatic" signifies one syllable sung to five or more notes of a melody. It is very typical of melismatic passages to have a single syllable sung with many notes; one sees this especially in the Alleluia of the Mass.

as tropes, in which a pre-existing chant melody, particularly a highly melismatic one, was given a new text, or a new melody was added to the one already existing. Overall, the entire chant development can be described as one of simple melody gradually becoming more and more elaborate. Moreover, it should be emphasized, just like the development of the Tridentine Mass, the chant was gradually and organically developed under the inspiration of orthodox Catholicism – and was not a series of hackneyed innovations coming from some half-baked liturgical committee.

By at least the ninth century (and probably earlier) composers also began experimenting with an idea that would be a logical extension of the concept of greater melodic elaboration. This idea consisted of an attempt to combine two or more of these extraordinarily beautiful melodies at the same time, while retaining a harmonious blend. Thus, with this principle, polyphony develops by reason of the simple desire to combine two or more chants and/or chant-like melodies at the same time into a harmonious whole – a logical extension of the chant principle of ever-expanding melodic elaboration.

Nevertheless, the idea of juxtaposing two or more chant melodies was fraught with major difficulties, for if one combined two pre-existing chant melodies at the same time, the resulting dissonances would clash, and consequently create a cacophonous din that would spoil the calm, consonant, and peaceful chant. Thus, the first obstacle to overcome was to find a way to combine chant melodies while maintaining a *harmonious* whole. The task was difficult because there was no systematic body of knowledge known as "counterpoint" in our understanding of the term. That is, there was no art of combining two or more melodies at the same time while maintaining a harmonious whole. This art had to be invented! Its development took painstaking, systematic experimentation over many centuries, and in several major stages. (This is, in a microcosm, the history and development of Western music, a music that was born from the womb of the Church.) Although the development is far too complex to examine here in detail, by about the middle of the fifteenth century classical polyphony had developed to the extent that it was ready to be brought to its maximum perfection by Flemish and then Roman (and other) composers of the sixteenth century.

There was also one other difficulty to overcome in this great development. It concerned the ability of the composer to maintain the style, feeling, and movement of the chant in the individual melodies of the polyphonic complex. This was accomplished by what today modern scholars call "borrowing procedures." In the earliest stages of this development, composers of polyphony would borrow an actual Gregorian chant melody (which was known as a *cantus firmus*, literally, a "fixed song") as a basis for a newly composed upper (or lower) part. The new melody both harmonized with, and was melodically very similar to, the *cantus firmus* chant tune. By this means, composers could use a true Gregorian melody, preserve the basic modes of the chant, and write a counterpoint of newly composed melodies that resembled the borrowed chant tune in style, feeling, and movement, all within a harmonious whole. One could not ask for a greater, more truly organic development from the chant.

As polyphonic sacred music continued to develop, composers gradually added more parts in counterpoint to the *cantus firmus*. As the texture of polyphony increased in complexity—to three, four, and even more voice parts—so did the sophistication of the borrowing procedures. By the fifteenth century, besides continuing to utilize *cantus firmus* technique, composers developed a new borrowing procedure known today as "paraphrase."

Paraphrase procedure involved borrowing a true Gregorian chant melody, but varying it by means of musical ornamentation. Whereas *cantus firmus* technique did not embellish the chant tune, and was principally used in only one voice part (i.e., either the soprano, alto, tenor, or bass), paraphrase would be utilized in several or even all voice parts with varied segments of the chant tune. It was often assisted by a technique known as "points of imitation" in which the varied chant melody set to the same text would be imitated in all the voice parts. In this way, a polyphonic composition would literally be permeated with variations, so to speak, of a real chant melody.

The culmination of all borrowing procedures occurs in the second half of the sixteenth century with the development of what is known today as "parody," or "imitatio" technique. Parody procedure involves borrowing whole segments of the polyphonic fabric of a composition, and then reworking and varying the melodies and harmonies comprising the texture. It could entail keeping the music largely intact (with only a few minor variations), and simply changing the words of the text to those of the new composition. It would more often involve rearranging the polyphonic texture in new ways; at the other extreme, the technique could involve a kind of "remote" parody that resembles paraphrase technique, but utilized various melodies from the model composition. Parody technique was most often used to compose Mass settings, where a motet (or other composition) would be used as a source or model. The Mass setting would thus consist of mostly music borrowed from the model composition, as well as a certain amount of newly composed music that retained the ethos of the music in the model. Masses that utilize this procedure are known today as "Parody Masses," or

"Imitatio Masses."[17] Parody technique, especially as used in the Mass, reaches its culmination in the late sixteenth century with the great European masters of classical polyphony, including the Roman school and, of course, many of the Masses of Giovanni Pierluigi da Palestrina.

A truly masterful example of these borrowing procedures shown in all of their variety occurs in the great Mass by Palestrina known as the *Missa Veni Sponsa Christi*. If Palestrina wrote only this composition, his fame in music history would be assured. This is a Parody Mass based on a motet of the same name composed by Palestrina. The motet, in turn, is itself based on a Gregorian chant melody "Veni Sponsa Christi."[18] The Latin of this beautiful text, along with my very literal translation, is as follows:

Veni Sponsa Christi,	Come, bride of Christ,
accipe coronam,	accept the crown
quam tibi Dominus,	which for you the Lord
praeparavit in aeternum.	has prepared for all eternity.
Alleluia.	Alleluia.

There are four phrases of the chant tune corresponding to the four divisions of the text. In his motet, Palestrina

---

[17] Patrick J. Brill, *The Parody Masses of Tomás Luis de Victoria*, Ph.D. Dissertation, University of Kansas, 1995, pp. 11–23. The designation "Parody Mass" does not signify or imply, in any way, that there is anything profane, irreverent, or blasphemous about these compositions. The word "parody" in this context refers only to a sixteenth-century compositional technique that denotes a type of borrowing procedure in which parts, or even whole sections, of a separate polyphonic composition are borrowed, and then reworked and varied in the Mass setting. Contemporary musicologists, being understandably uncomfortable with the term "parody," have come up with a substitute word, "imitation," or "*imitatio*" procedure. However, this term is very misleading in that it also refers to several different types of contrapuntal procedures that are not part of sixteenth-century parody procedure. Therefore, neither term is particularly good.
[18] *Liber Usualis*, with introduction and rubrics in English, ed. Benedictines of Solesmes (Tournai: Desclée, 1952), 1214.

takes the first chant segment on the text "Veni Sponsa Christi," and sets it to points of imitation occurring successively in all four voice parts (SATB). The chant tune has also been varied with beautiful ornaments that adorn the original melody, but do not aurally obscure it. Palestrina takes the next chant segment on "accipe coronam," and composes a new set of points of imitation (that are also varied versions of the chant) in each of the four voices. This set of points of imitation is skillfully dovetailed with the end of the preceding set of points of imitation on "Veni sponsa Christi." Palestrina then does the same with "quam tibi Dominus," as well as the segment on "praeparavit in aeternum." Thus, the entire composition consists of an uninterrupted succession of points of imitation using each text segment melody that has been varied and presented in the order found in the original chant melody. By these paraphrase and imitative techniques, Palestrina imbues the entire motet with variants of a single chant melody in a mystical and harmonious whole.

However, Palestrina is not yet finished. Utilizing parody technique, he then takes large portions of the actual contrapuntal texture of his "Veni Sponsa Christi" motet, and uses these parts as a basis for composing an entire setting of the Mass, *Missa Veni Sponsa Christi.* In his use of parody procedure, Palestrina utilizes the standard Ordinary texts of the Mass – that is, the Kyrie, Gloria, Credo, Sanctus/Benedictus, and Agnus Dei – and sets these texts to variations, or the "reworking," so to speak, of portions of the polyphonic music from the motet. While he will occasionally include music that is not directly derived from the motet in the Mass, this newly composed music will nonetheless have the "flavor and feel" of the original melodies in the motet. Thus, the Mass is thoroughly imbued with a kaleidoscope of variants from the motet, as well as elements of the original chant melody, all within a harmonious and mystical whole.

In summary, by means of these various borrowing procedures, the original chant tune has now been amplified and expanded into a full-scale Mass that is permeated with the sense of the sacred, mystical harmonies, and melodies that have the movement, feel, and style of the Gregorian chant. This is what Pius means in the *Votum* when he writes that the classical polyphony is "inspired by Gregorian chant."[19] Is it thus any wonder that Pius lauds this kind of music?

We can conclude from the above that the classical polyphony is *posterior* to the chant in that it is the *result*, the *effect* if you will, of a long and painstaking process of organic development *from* the chant, and not the reverse; that the late classical polyphony is a magnificent amplification and variation, as well as the logical result, of the various musical processes of expansion and elaboration which utilize Gregorian chant as their proper matter and starting point.

Now since the chant is "prior" to the polyphony, and the word "prior" can be used in several senses, one can inquire which meanings of "prior" are operative here. In his work, the *Categories*, Aristotle writes that there are five senses of the word "prior"; we will only be concerned with three of these senses.

> Primarily and most properly the term has reference to time: in this sense the word is used to indicate that one thing is older or more ancient than another, for the expressions "older" and "more ancient" imply greater length of time.
>
> Secondly, one thing is said to be "prior" to another when the sequence of their being cannot

---

[19] Part I: General Considerations, *Votum* of 1893 as quoted in PLSM 206.

be reversed. In this sense "one" is "prior" to "two."
For if "two" exists, it follows directly that "one"
must exist, but if "one" exists, it does not follow
necessarily that "two" exists: thus the sequence
subsisting cannot be reversed. It is agreed, then,
that when the sequence of two things cannot
be reversed, then that one on which the other
depends is called "prior" to that other.

Yet it would seem that besides those mentioned there is yet another. For in those things,
the being of each of which implies that of the
other, that which is in any way the cause may
reasonably be said to be by nature "prior" to the
effect.[20]

Thus, Gregorian chant is prior to the classical polyphony in the first sense which Aristotle describes, because
chant is certainly "more ancient" than polyphony. It is
also prior to classical polyphony in the second sense,
because the emergence of classical polyphony is the result
of an organic development *from* the chant, but *not the
reverse*. In the third sense, the chant is prior to sacred
polyphony in that the chant is a sort of material cause,
and polyphony is an effect, of the borrowing processes
that utilize Gregorian chant melodies.

With this historical background, we can now answer
the questions raised above regarding Pius's understanding
of the relationships between chant and polyphony, as
well as the question of why classical polyphony is not
the highest model of all sacred music.

From the examination above, it is clear that with
regard to *place*, Gregorian chant holds a clear "pride of
place," and is thus the highest model of sacred music in
the liturgy for the following reasons:

---

[20] Aristotle, *Categories*, in *The Basic Works of Aristotle*, ed. Richard
McKeon (New York: Random House, 1941), 34.

1. The chant has been inherited from the ancient Fathers of the Church. (Priority of time)
2. It is the only chant that has been kept by the Church over the centuries in her actual liturgical books.
3. It is the only music that the Church offers to the faithful as her very own music.
4. There are still certain texts that may be sung only in chant (Epistle, Gospel, and other High Mass texts).
5. Chant is prior to the sacred polyphony because the sequence of their being cannot be reversed, for sacred polyphony is truly an organic development *from* the chant, and *not the reverse*.
6. Chant has a sort of causal priority in that it comprises, in a way, the matter of sacred polyphony, so that (at least when borrowing procedures utilizing chant are operative) the being of sacred polyphony truly originates from that of the sacred chant.

It does not follow from the above, however, that classical polyphony is *inferior* to the chant with respect to the *degree* to which sacred polyphony is endowed with the three qualities of sacred music—art, holiness, and universality. On the contrary, classical polyphony is on the same level as the chant in this regard, for the following reasons given by Pius X himself:

1. Per the *Votum* (as quoted earlier), Pius declares that both chant and classical polyphony correspond "fully and perfectly to the three qualities of sacred music which we mentioned above."
2. Per also the *Votum*, Pius declares that sacred polyphony is "so truly fitting as to stand side by side with Gregorian chant."[21]

---

[21] Part I: General Considerations, *Votum* of 1893 as quoted in PLSM 206.

Although these quotations should settle the issue, one might object to the above conclusion by arguing that in both Instructions – from the *Votum*, and from the motu proprio of 1903 – it is written that the three qualities of sacred music are found "most perfectly in Gregorian chant," and "to a high degree in music of the classical school." This would seem to imply that polyphony is also inferior to the chant regarding these three qualities. Nevertheless, in Part I of the *Votum* (entitled: "General Considerations"), as we saw above, Pius declares that *both* chant and sacred polyphony correspond "fully and perfectly" to the three qualities of sacred music. These are Pius's own words. [22] Now unless Pius is contradicting himself, or had somehow changed his mind before finishing the *Votum* (both very unlikely), it follows that classical polyphony is indeed equal to chant insofar as it is endowed with the three qualities of sacred music. It also, incidentally, underscores the importance of reading all of the major documents on sacred music by Pius X.

It should be added that, unlike modern music, only chant and classical polyphony can be regarded as true *models* of Catholic sacred music, because again, both chant and sacred polyphony conform "fully and perfectly" to the three qualities of sacred music.

Pius next turns to the *third* kind of sacred music, namely, modern music:

---

[22] The expressions "most perfectly," and "to a high degree" in the original Italian confirm Pius's meaning: for chant, Pius uses the Italian phrase *"in grado sommo,"* which literally translates "in the highest degree." For classical polyphony he uses the phrase *"in ottimo grado,"* which literally translates "in a perfect degree." Hayburn's translation consequently misses the note of perfection in Pius's thoughts on polyphony vs. chant, and inadvertently causes his readers to misread Pius's meaning. Thus, in the original language, Pius is expressing the equality of the two exemplars insofar as they have the three qualities of sacred music to a perfect degree. He is just using slightly different, but equivalent, Italian expressions.

5. The Church has always recognised and encouraged all progress in the arts, and has always admitted to the service of her functions whatever is good and beautiful in their development during different centuries, as long as they do not offend against the laws of her liturgy. Hence more modern music may also be allowed in churches, since it has produced compositions good and serious and dignified enough to be worthy of liturgical use.

Nevertheless, since modern music has become chiefly a secular art, greater care must be taken, when admitting it, that nothing profane be allowed, nothing that is reminiscent of theatrical pieces, nothing based as to its form on the style of secular compositions.

6. Among all kinds of modern music the theatrical style that was so much in vogue during the last century, for instance, in Italy, is the one least fitted to accompany the service of the Church. This style is by nature the most unlike Gregorian chant and the music of the classical school, and therefore the least compatible with the laws of good sacred music. Moreover, the rhythm, the structure, and the convention of this style do not lend themselves well to the demands of really liturgical music.[23]

In the first paragraph of no. 5, Pius repeats the constant claims of the Church that it recognizes and encourages all progress in the arts. This has been exemplified by the admission of appropriate modern compositions into the liturgy. By "appropriate" is meant modern music that comes close in its expression, feeling, and movement to the two exemplars of sacred music, namely, chant and classical polyphony. By "modern music" Pius is referring to sacred music from the seventeenth century to Pius's

---

[23] Motu proprio of 1903 as quoted in PLSM 225–26. Hereafter, "MP in PLSM."

own time. Pius also recognizes that composers of modern music have "produced compositions good and serious and dignified enough to be worthy of liturgical use."

The second paragraph cautions music directors that since modern music has become mostly a secular art, greater care must be exercised in choosing modern compositions to ensure that they contain nothing of the profane, no theatrical ethos, and nothing based on the forms of secular music.

The paragraph that makes up no. 6 is very clear; for Pius the theatrical style is the least suitable for sacred music. Pius explains this very well, and there is no need to give a detailed commentary. The only caveat I would add is that while Pius very clearly puts the "theatrical style" on the top of his black list, Pius never heard "rock 'n' roll," much less the blatantly satanic "heavy metal" music that is so popular today. Thus, it is crucial to understand that in these paragraphs he is proscribing *any* kind of secular or profane music for use in the liturgy, including "popular," secular, sentimental, theatrical, and yes, we can safely say by implication, "rock 'n' roll" music and its various offshoots. This also underscores the utter fatuity of attempting to bring into the liturgy such things as "Christian rock," or for that matter, the adoption of any kind of "rock" or "pop" music in the liturgy by setting sacred texts to profane music. When one does this, he is committing at least material *sacrilege* and *blasphemy*.[24]

At this point, we will summarize our findings, and then continue to explore, by way of commentary, the principles in the motu proprio. However, first, it is incumbent to point out some of the main obstacles to

---

[24] For a thorough critique of rock and pop music, see Peter A. Kwasniewski, *Good Music, Sacred Music, and Silence: Three Gifts of God for Liturgy and for Life* (Gastonia, NC: TAN Books, 2023), 24–54.

understanding Pius X's legislation, since without some knowledge of the pitfalls of interpreting ecclesiastical documents, one could easily misunderstand the mind of this great and holy pope.

CAVEATS

First, it is crucial to understand that this motu proprio is a normative summation of the principles of Catholic sacred music. It is normative in that it is concerned primarily with legislative norms – not complex exceptional circumstances. It is a summation in the sense that it treats the subject principally in general terms, and, with just a few exceptions, avoids extensive and detailed discussions. It is also not a formal treatise, even though it contains occasional technical language.

Second, there is a tendency, today, to interpret ecclesiastical documents out of their proper contexts. These include musical, liturgical, as well as theological, canonical, and historical contexts. This would happen, for example, if one were to conclude that Pius would consider contemporary "rock 'n' roll" music to be better than nineteenth-century "theatrical music," because Pius states that: "This [theatrical] style is by nature the most unlike Gregorian chant and music of the classical school, and therefore the least compatible with the laws of good sacred music." It would truly be an example of an interpretation taken out of its proper historical context, since Pius never heard contemporary "rock 'n' roll," or its various derivatives. But since "rock music" is far more antithetical to Catholic sacred music than virtually any of the "theatrical" compositions of Pius's day, Pius, based on the principles of his own legislation, would most definitely have considered contemporary "rock 'n' roll," especially as applied to liturgical music, to be far worse than late nineteenth-century operatic music.

Third, one should also be careful to avoid a too "legalistic" interpretation of Pius's motu proprio. This would entail reading the document as if there were no need to interpret the legislation, as well as assuming that it contained the last legal word on all aspects of sacred music, including the many unexpressed or implicit exceptions to general rules.

By way of illustration, one of the best examples of a non-musical Church document that is frequently abused today by faulty "conservative" Catholic interpretations based on contextual errors is *Pastor Aeternus*, the Vatican I document that contains the infallible definition of papal magisterial and jurisdictional authority. If one were to read this document without knowing its proper historical, theological, and canonical contexts, it would be very easy to construe the section on jurisdictional primacy as asserting that papal authority is absolute and without qualification. Contemporary "conservative" Catholics, reading it out of context, interpret it in a legalistic way, claiming that papal authority is absolute and without exception – that a pope could introduce any change in doctrine and practice, even if it contradicts previous consistent papal teaching. This is the basis of the error of papolatry, and reveals a true ignorance of the contextual details surrounding the definition of papal primacy.[25] Because of

---

[25] When a General Council prepares to define solemnly a doctrine using the extraordinary infallible Magisterium, a committee of cardinal-theologians known as the "Deputation of the Faith" is convened and charged with the correct interpretation of the doctrines, as well as the composition of documents containing the correct and official written expression of those doctrines. The drafts of these documents are called "schemas," and are circulated to the Council Fathers for their input, criticisms, questions, and the like. When the Council Fathers execute their final vote, this interpretation of the Deputation of the Faith becomes, *ex post facto*, the Church's official interpretation.

Now before the final vote on *Pastor Aeternus* at Vatican I, several Council Fathers were concerned that they would be voting for a

this, contemporary traditionalists must endure not only
the madness of a "liberal" Catholic apostasy run amuck

---

doctrine that would give the pope absolute and unqualified jurisdictional authority. Various (documented) discussions were given
by members of the Deputation of the Faith assuring the Council
Fathers that this was *not* a correct understanding of the doctrine.
That is, they (the Relators [i.e., spokesmen] of the Deputation)
stated that the pope, in his jurisdictional authority, does *not* have
absolute and unqualified jurisdictional authority. One Council
Father, however, an American named Bishop Verot of Savannah,
apparently was not convinced, and requested that specific qualify-
ing statements (to the effect that the pope's jurisdictional authority
is qualified) be inserted into the texts of the schemas. He was told
that the Council Fathers had not come to Rome "to hear buffooneries." In other words, if this bishop had understood the theological
context of the *schema*, he would not have put himself in such an
embarrassing situation. See Michael Davies, *Pope Paul's New Mass*
(Kansas City, MO: The Angelus Press, 2009), 631–45, esp. 635–36.

Furthermore, in describing the obedience due to the pope in
jurisdictional matters, the text of *Pastor Aeternus* uses the Latin
phrase "*vera obedientia*," which literally translates: "true obedience." Anyone familiar with St. Thomas Aquinas knows that this
is alluding to the three kinds of obedience the Angelic Doctor refers
to in his own discussion of obedience in the *Summa theologiae* (II-II,
Q. 104, art. 5, especially ad 3). These three kinds are: true obedience, which suffices for salvation; perfect obedience, in which one
obeys in all things lawful; and false obedience, in which one obeys
even in things unlawful. From this, it is clear that the context of
Pastor Aeternus is that of *true obedience*, and is not commanding
us to obey the pope when he orders something that is unlawful. In
other words, there are certain *conditions of validity* that the pope
must respect when issuing any binding order. Thus, if he issues
any command that strays outside the bounds of these conditions,
his subjects are not *required* to obey him. Moreover, if he were
to command his subjects to commit an offense against God, his
subjects would be *obligated* to ignore him.

Some might object to this interpretation and cite St. Paul where
he states: "Children, obey your parents *in all things*," and in verse
22, "Servants obey *in all things* your masters according to the flesh"
(Col. 3:20–22). However, St. Thomas, in his reply to this very
objection (II-II, Q. 104, art. 5, ad 1), states: "When the Apostle says
'in all things,' he refers to matters within the sphere of a father's
or master's authority." Thus, Christian authority, including papal
jurisdictional authority, must remain within its proper sphere,
and therefore is not absolute in an unqualified sense.

on the one hand, but also the sad spectacle of "conservative" Catholic buffooneries on the other.

RECAPITULATION AND SUMMARY OF THE PRINCIPLES ARTICULATED THUS FAR

Recapitulating the principles of the reform discussed thus far, Pius begins his motu proprio of 1903 with an introduction that initiates a discussion of the grave duties of the supreme pontiff in safeguarding the liturgy from any kind of profanation. He next raises the problem of the many sacred music abuses occurring in the Catholic Church, thus articulating the central problem of the reform. He ends the Introduction with a formal exhortation to follow all of the precepts outlined in the document. The exhortation contains a reminder that the document has the force of a genuine canonical code on music for the universal Church.

In the second part, the Instruction on Sacred Music, I. General Principles, Pius begins by articulating the purposes of sacred music. These include the honor and glory of God, as well as adorning the sacred texts with great and lofty melodies, which in turn inspire the congregation to greater devotion. This greater devotion leads the congregation to be better disposed to the abundance of graces at the traditional Mass.

Pius then takes up the three qualities of the liturgy that all sacred music must possess, namely, holiness, art, and universality. Each of these qualities is described and exemplified. It is stressed that ONLY music with all three of these qualities, with no hint of the secular either in itself or in the way that it is performed, may be admitted into the liturgy.

In section II, Various Kinds of Sacred Music, Pius introduces us to the three types of sacred music that may be used in the Catholic liturgy, namely, Gregorian chant, classical polyphony, and appropriate types of modern sacred music. Chant has pride of place and is the highest model of sacred music. Classical polyphony is also a model (after chant) of Catholic sacred music. Both chant and classical polyphony "fully and perfectly" exemplify the qualities of holiness, art, and universality. Polyphonic sacred music is best represented in the late sixteenth-century Roman school, particularly the music of the greatest of the Roman school composers, Giovanni Pierluigi da Palestrina. Modern sacred music can be used in the liturgy with certain reservations, that is, provided the music is devoid of any secular elements and resembles the chant and classical polyphony in its movement, style, and mysticism. This is because modern music is mostly a secular art (indeed, in some cases today, a satanic art), and thus greater care is needed in choosing an appropriate piece of modern sacred music for the liturgy. Even though modern music may be used in the liturgy, it is not an exemplar of Catholic sacred music.

CHAPTER 3
Continuation of "The Instruction on Sacred Music"

THE LITURGICAL TEXT

> 7. The language of the Roman Church is Latin. It is therefore forbidden to sing anything in the vulgar tongue during solemn liturgical functions, and much more is it forbidden to sing in the vulgar tongue the parts, either proper or common, of the Mass and the Divine Office. [1]

Indeed, the language of the Western Church *is* Latin. Here is the wisdom of Pope St. Pius X; all one needs to do is observe the sacrilegious travesty that is the *Novus Ordo Missae* to see what happens when this rule is ignored, and replaced by vernacular translations that render the theology of the Mass ambiguous. The neo-Modernist reformers, of course, knew that by destroying the Latin, they would also destroy the treasury of sacred music at the same time. As contemporary traditional Catholic readers have known for years, the destruction of Latin was accomplished by official documents that appeared on the surface to call for the retention of Latin. This is because the revolutionaries at Vatican II deliberately inserted loopholes that undercut the very legislation the documents were supposed to

---

[1] MP in PLSM 226.

uphold.[2] Thus, with the mandatory use of Latin effectively overruled, there was no need to retain traditional sacred music, most of which was set to Latin texts.

Pius also forbids the singing of anything in the vernacular "during solemn liturgical functions." Here Pius means that once the liturgy has begun, and until it has ended, no vernacular music should be heard. In the context of a Mass, however, it is permissible to sing a sacred composition in the vernacular *before* the Mass begins (usually as a processional), and then to sing one *after* Mass is over (normally as a recessional).[3] It is strictly forbidden to sing anything from the Proper or the Ordinary of either the Mass or Divine Office in the vernacular, because these are all *integral parts* of a sung Latin liturgy.

> 8. Since the text to be sung and the order in which it is to be sung are already determined for every liturgical service, it is not lawful to change either the words or their order, nor to substitute another text, nor to leave anything out, either entirely or in part, except in the cases in which the rubrics allow the organ alone to replace certain verses which must then be recited in the choir. It is only allowed, according to the custom of the Roman Church, to sing a Motet in honor of the Blessed Sacrament after the Benedictus at High Mass. A short Motet with words approved by the Church may also be added after the proper Offertory of the Mass has been sung.[4]

These rules prohibit any change in the order of the text, changes in the words themselves, and all omissions or additions (even partial ones) of the sacred texts. These

---

[2] Patrick J. Brill, "The Tridentine Mass and the Treasury of Catholic Sacred Music," *The Remnant*, July 31, 1991.
[3] These vernacular compositions must still possess all three qualities of sacred music.
[4] MP in PLSM 226.

regulations are aimed primarily at musicians in Pius's day that would make theatrical songs out of liturgical texts.

Singing a motet in honor of the Blessed Sacrament "after the Benedictus at High Mass" is a time-honored custom. A short motet may also be added during the Offertory *after* the Offertory Proper is sung. These latter are often motets with Marian texts in honor of the Blessed Virgin Mary. Motets sung during the Offertory are best completed by the time the priest proclaims the *Orate Fratres*.

> 9. The liturgical text must be sung just as it stands in the authentic books, without changing or transposing the words, without needless repetition, without dividing the syllables, and always so that it can be understood by the people who hear it.[5]

These rules partly reinforce those of no. 8. They also add the prohibition against excessive repetition of the words of the text, as well as ensuring that the text is always clearly audible to the congregation, a principle that was much stressed in the discussions at the Council of Trent.[6] This section is also probably alluding to the shoddy practice of composers and arrangers who would divide the syllables in non-traditional ways, and then obscure the intelligibility of the text with excessive repetitions and unconventional syllabic divisions in order to set sacred texts to operatic style melodies.

THE EXTERNAL FORM OF SACRED MUSIC

> 10. Each part of the Mass and the Divine Office must keep, even in the music, that form and character which it has from tradition, and which is very well expressed in Gregorian

---

[5] PLSM 227.
[6] See Craig A. Monson, "The Council of Trent Revisited," *Journal of the American Musicological Society*, vol. 55, no. 1 (2002): 1–37.

chant. Therefore, Introits, Graduals, antiphons, psalms, hymns, the Gloria in excelsis, etc., will be composed each in their own way.[7]

This paragraph points to the importance of retaining the traditional textual forms of the liturgy, as well as the basic musical styles of the various types of chant, in polyphonic compositions. Each chant type, such as the Introit for example, has a traditional textual form, as well as its traditional musical setting that is based on that textual form. The textual form of the Introit consists of an antiphon text that precedes a single verse of a psalm followed by the *Gloria Patri*. After the psalm and the *Gloria Patri*, the antiphon text is then repeated exactly. Thus, the textual form is A B A.[8]

The typical Gregorian chant setting of the Introit text also follows this form, and utilizes the traditional stylistic features associated with each part of the Introit. For example, the chant setting of an antiphon has a melodic style suited to the use of antiphon texts, which means that it is short in time, neumatic in style, normal in range, and rather melodious. On the other hand, the psalm setting of the verse and the *Gloria Patri* exhibits the musical *psalmodic* style with its narrow range, *co-finalis* reciting tone, many repeated notes, and characteristic *mediatio* and *terminatio* cadences, all virtually identical to the treatment of psalms in the Divine Office.[9] Then the musical antiphon, exactly as found in the beginning, will be repeated. Thus, the musical form is also A B A. The point of this paragraph is that polyphonic compositions that set sacred liturgical

---

[7] PLSM 227.

[8] That is, if we take the verse together with the doxology in contrast to the neumatic antiphon that precedes and succeeds it.

[9] In the psalms of the Divine Office, the antiphon is followed by many verses of the psalm, and is punctuated by the lesser doxology. Then the antiphon is repeated. Thus, the Introit has its roots in psalm singing.

texts should exhibit only the traditional forms and styles of the musical parts of the Mass and the Divine Office.

This rule also applies to new compositions that set any of the above-mentioned types. Thus, composers are exhorted to respect the traditional forms and musical styles of these chant types and their texts.

> 11. Especially must these rules be followed:
> a) The Kyrie, Gloria, Credo, etc., of the Mass must represent in the music the unity of their text. They may not be made up of separate pieces, each of which forms a complete musical composition which could be taken away from the others and followed by something quite different. [10]

In this section, Pius legislates against a common practice that first rose to prominence in the Baroque period and became pervasive in the orchestral Masses of the eighteenth and nineteenth centuries, namely, the division of a single part of the Mass Ordinary into multiple distinct, stand-alone movements — say, the Kyrie divided into three movements of contrasting keys, tempos, and forces; the Gloria or the Credo into half-a-dozen movements; the Agnus Dei into two movements (for examples, see Bach's *Mass in B Minor*, Vivaldi's *Gloria*, Mozart's *Great Mass in C Minor*, or Haydn's *Theresienmesse*). Since the movements are independent (not forming a single musical whole like a Gregorian Kyrie or a piece of classical polyphony in which the textual unity is respected amidst whatever subdivisions there may be), *in theory* different pieces could be substituted for those individual movements, if the style or key relationship made sense. This kind of treatment of the liturgical text risks weakening the unity of the prayer offered by the Church; the composition seems to lack integrity of form for its purpose. In

---

[10] MP in PLSM 227.

addition, Pius X may be pointing to the desirable quality of musical integration within each movement and across the movements by means of, say, the use of the same Gregorian *cantus firmus* or by utilizing related musical motifs and harmonies. Such techniques bestow organic unity on the movements and upon the polyphonic Mass setting as a whole, which is symbolically appropriate for the offering of a single sacrifice, spiritually beneficial by highlighting the unity of the Mass in musical terms, and practically advantageous for singers who are learning the material.

> b) At Vespers the ordinary rule must be that of the *Caeremoniale Episcoporum*, which requires Gregorian chant for the psalms and allows figured music for the verses of the Gloria Patri and the hymn.
>
> Nevertheless on great feasts Gregorian chant may be used in turn with a so-called falso bordone chant, or with verses composed in the same suitable style.
>
> It may even be allowed to sing a whole psalm in figured music sometimes, as long as the proper form of singing psalms is not lost, that is, as long as the singers really appear to be changing verses alternately, either with new melodies or with those taken from or modeled on Gregorian chant. Psalms sung in the manner called *di concerto* are therefore absolutely forbidden.[11]

Here Pius reiterates the general principle found in the *Ceremonial of Bishops* for Vespers.[12] This rule requires

---

[11] PLSM 227.

[12] The *Ceremonial of Bishops* (*Caeremoniale Episcoporum*) is a compilation of ritual directions for the liturgical functions of a bishop during Mass, the Divine Office, and other liturgies. The *Ceremonial* consists of three books, which, it should be noted, do not contain liturgical texts, but only directions for bishops on what procedures to follow during these liturgies. The *Ceremonial* also contains many references to the laws of sacred music, including directions addressed to organists, singers, and choirmasters.

psalms themselves to be chanted, but also permits, as an option, the use of "figured music" (that is, polyphonic music of either the classical school, or appropriate modern compositions) to substitute for the chant on the verses of the lesser doxology and hymn. Moreover, on "great feasts" the Gregorian chant may also be adapted to a "so-called *falso bordone* chant." The Italian term *falso bordone*, literally translated, means "false bass," and is a technical term that refers to a chant melody set in four-part harmony that retains the declamatory style of the chant.[13]

In the second paragraph of no. 11 (b), Pius adds an exception to the rule found in the *Ceremonial* by allowing an entire psalm to be sung in figured music as long as the correct form of psalm singing is observed. In terms of form, Pius is alluding primarily to what is known as the "antiphonal style" of singing, that is, one psalm verse sung by one section of the choir alternating with the next verse, which is then sung by the other section of the choir, and so on. Psalm settings can be done with new melodies, melodies taken from chant, or those modeled on chant.

Pius further prohibits the use of the "*di concerto*" style for the setting of psalms. The "*di concerto*" style, or as it is usually termed today, the "concerted style," refers, in a more restricted sense, to music in which soloists contend, or compete with, the other instruments in the ensemble. In a broader sense, it signifies the conventional styles and sub-genres typically used in Western opera, such as the

---

[13] *Falso bordone* should not be confused with the word "*fauxbourdon*," which latter term signifies a fifteenth-century French compositional technique that consists of a Gregorian chant melody transposed an octave higher, and which is then doubled a sixth below with a middle part improvised a fourth below the chant tune. In modern terminology, *fauxbourdon* amounts to a series of three-part parallel sixth chords based on a Gregorian chant melody. Technically, the four-part harmony of the *falso bordone* consists of triadic harmonies with conventional doublings, to create a four-part homophonic texture.

recitative, aria, arioso, chorus, ensemble, and the like. This regulation, of course, follows logically enough from Pius's prohibition of the use of theatrical conventions in sacred music, as well as his respect for the traditional form of the Catholic psalm.[14]

> c) The hymns of the Church must also keep their traditional form. It is not lawful, for instance, to compose a *Tantum Ergo* so that the first verse be a romance, an air or an adagio, and then the *Genitori* an allegro.[15]

Paragraph c is a corollary of no. 10 above, but with special emphasis on the traditional form of the hymn. Here Pius exemplifies the rule with the well-known hymn from the Benediction of the Blessed Sacrament, *Tantum Ergo*, which itself is divided into two verses that begin with the following texts: *Tantum Ergo* and *Genitori*. Pius cautions composers not to set the first verse in the manner of a "romance," "air," or "adagio," followed by an "allegro" on the next verse, *Genitori*.

---

[14] The term "*di concerto*" style, in the more restricted sense, indicates a style originally derived from Baroque concerted genres, such as the concerto grosso, solo concerto, and the like. In this style, a soloist (or small group of soloists) will "compete" or "contend" in the sense that the soloist will often have musical themes that are different from those in the orchestra, or "tutti" sections of a concerto. In Baroque concerted music, the soloist's themes will often be in stark contrast to the thematic material of the orchestra, and will often be developed somewhat independently of the orchestral material as well. This style would thus not be appropriate to the singing of traditional Catholic psalms, since Catholic psalms are sung in an alternating "antiphonal style" in which the psalm melody remains virtually constant. In the broader sense, "*di concerto*" style can be applied to operatic sub-genres such as the aria, recitative, chorus, and the like. Here the sense is a solo melody that has an accompaniment, often elaborate, that conveys contrast in a way similar to the stricter sense of "*di concerto*" style. This style would also be inappropriate to the traditional Catholic psalm for the same reason cited above. Pius appears to be using the term in its broader sense.

[15] MP in PLSM 227.

A "romance" (*Romanze* in German), as used in nineteenth-century musical parlance, often indicates a short, lyrical composition for piano, or for solo instrument with piano accompaniment. However, in Pius's day the solo instrument of a romance could also be the human voice. These vocal romances are most often found in operas of the nineteenth century. It appears that Pius is alluding here to vocal romances, as well as typical vocal operatic solo sub-genres, such as "airs" and "adagios." Each of these would normally be taken at a rather slow tempo. An "allegro," on the other hand, was a composition in a faster tempo, especially like those in the first and last movements of a typical sonata or symphony. The extreme contrast that would thus result using a "romance," "air," or "adagio" for the *Tantum Ergo*, only to be followed by a much faster "allegro" on the *Genitori*, would be out of character for the traditional hymn, which keeps the same basic melody and tempo for each of its verses. Moreover, these nineteenth-century genres would not be suitable to a hymn because they are not normally associated with the generally syllabic style of the traditional Catholic hymn.[16]

> d) The antiphons at Vespers should ordinarily be sung to their own Gregorian chant. If, for any special reason, they are sung to modern music, the melody must never be like an air in a concert, or as long as a motet or a song.[17]

---

[16] The term "romance" is admittedly rather vague. In the 1908 edition of *Grove's Dictionary of Music and Musicians* (which was published during Pius's pontificate), a *romance* is defined as: "A term of very vague signification, answering in music to the same term in poetry, where the characteristics are rather those of personal sentiment and expression than of precise form." Undoubtedly Pius also disliked the romance because of its sentimental character, which character was opposed to the sense of the sacred.

[17] MP in PLSM 227.

Pius adds this note concerning antiphons at Vespers in order to reaffirm the general and preferable use of Gregorian chant for the antiphon that precedes the verses of a particular psalm. In the exceptional event of the use of modern music instead of the chant, the antiphon melody must never resemble an "air," that is, it must not resemble an operatic "aria," or "arioso," to use the proper Italian operatic terms. This again is to keep the theatrical style out of the liturgy, and to preserve the traditional style of psalmody. Pius also mentions the proscription against music that is as long as a motet or a song. Here Pius desires that the antiphons of Vespers be in keeping with the brevity of the Gregorian chant antiphons traditionally used at Vespers.

THE SINGERS

> 12. Except the chant of the celebrant and the sacred ministers at the altar, which must always be sung in Gregorian chant without any accompaniment, the rest of the liturgical singing belongs properly to the choir of clerics: wherefore singers in church, if they are laymen, are the substitutes of the ecclesiastical choir. Hence, their music, at any rate for the greater part, must keep the nature of choir music.
>
> This does not entirely exclude solos. But these must never take the chief place in a service, they should never absorb the greater part of the liturgical text; they must be rather points of musical emphasis and accent bound up closely with the rest of the composition which should remain strictly choral.[18]

---

[18] PLSM 228. The context here regarding solo singing is the High Mass. Given the crisis currently raging in the Church, as well as the severe shortage of properly qualified vocalists, I think that it is permissible to sing solo Gregorian chant at a Low Mass, if other qualified singers are not available.

The gist of the first paragraph in no. 12 is that, with the exception of the unaccompanied chant sung by the celebrant and the sacred ministers at the altar, the remaining liturgical singing "belongs properly to the choir of clerics." Since this is primarily a clerical function, if laymen are utilized in their stead, these laymen constitute "substitutes of the ecclesiastical choir." Here Pius is alluding to the fact that the use of laymen as substitutes is in reality a delegated ministry. Because of this, the music, for the most part, must be fundamentally choir music. Thus, instruments, including the organ, are *secondary* to the primarily vocal nature of Catholic sacred music.

In the second paragraph of no. 12, Pius informs us that even though sacred music is primarily choir music, it may be appropriate, at times, to include vocal solos. However, these solos must never be the primary focus of a liturgy, and should never take up the majority of the liturgical text; rather, they should be points of emphasis in a primarily choral expression of the liturgical texts. By the words "choral" and "choir" here, Pius means *many* choristers singing at the same time, as opposed to one singer (or at most two singers) singing a "solo."

> 13. It follows from the same principle that the singers in church have a real liturgical office, and that women, therefore, being incapable of such an office, cannot be admitted to the choir. If high voices, such as treble and alto, are wanted, these parts must be sung by boys, according to the ancient custom of the Church.[19]

Here is it important to recall our discussion of contexts earlier in chapter 2. As mentioned there, the motu proprio is a *normative summation* of the principles of sacred music. It is thus particularly important *not* to interpret

---

[19] PLSM 228.

this passage as indicating that women are absolutely, without exception, excluded from the choir. That would be too legalistic an interpretation. The fact is, Pius X *did* allow certain exceptions, and he says so himself in other official documents. For example, in the Instruction on Sacred Music from the *Votum* of 1893, he begins the *Votum*'s paragraph no. 13 *exactly* as quoted above in the motu proprio of 1903. But in the *Votum*, Pius also adds the following:

> In the case of groups of religious, and also those groups of religious which are congregations of women, it is permissible for them to sing those parts which belong to the choir, but only in churches and chapels of their own monasteries and institutions. [20]

In addition, there are other documents issued from the Sacred Congregation of Rites during the reign of Pius X, which, in the event that a choir director is unable to find adequately trained boys for the soprano and alto parts, do allow women in parish churches to sing these upper parts. [21]

> 14. Lastly, only men of known piety and integrity who, by their modest and reverent demeanor during the service, show themselves worthy of the sacred duty they perform, may be allowed to sing in the choir. It would also be more suitable if the singers, while they are in choir, were to wear cassocks and surplices; and if their place be too much exposed to the gaze of the people, it should be guarded by a grating. [22]

---

[20] PLSM 228. It is true that the *Votum* of 1893 was written before Pius became pope; nevertheless, the close correspondence of the *Votum* to the motu proprio of 1903 shows that Pius had not changed his mind on this matter.

[21] Cf. Peter Kwasniewski, "Are Women Permitted to Sing the Propers of the Mass?," *New Liturgical Movement*, March 8, 2021.

[22] PLSM 228.

This is self-explanatory, but unfortunately, many church choir singers today seem to forget where they are during rehearsals and even liturgies, namely, in the house of God. There they sing, laugh, talk, make fun of the conductor, and socialize, when they should be concentrating on music and prayer. This is a constant complaint of choir directors, and I, as a choir director myself, have occasionally experienced this kind of irreverence and disrespect in church by choristers, particularly at rehearsals. Unfortunately, singers often act as though they have completely forgotten that God just happens to be Existence Itself, who created the entire universe, both visible and invisible, and who sustains that universe (including their vocal chords) at every moment. They also seem to forget that that same God will judge solemnly every one of us at the end of our lives.

The reference to cassocks, surplices, and gratings applies to choirs that sing adjacent to the sanctuary, as did many choirs in the churches of Pius's day, especially in Europe. However, this rule should still apply today in those churches where choirs sing close to the sanctuary.

THE ORGAN AND OTHER INSTRUMENTS

> 15. Although the proper music of the Church is only vocal, nevertheless the accompaniment of an organ is allowed. In any special case, within proper limits and with due care, other instruments may be allowed too, but never without special leave from the Bishop of the Diocese, according to the rule of the *Caeremoniale Episcoporum.*[23]

The norm for sacred music is vocal, that is, vocal music is the first and truly "proper" music of the Church. The organ, secondary to vocal music, is the main non-vocal

---

[23] PLSM 228.

instrument used to accompany the singing, as well as to provide sustained vocal-like music when the singers are silent. Other musical instruments besides the organ are *exceptions* to the norm, and may not be used without special permission of the local Ordinary, as found in the rule of the *Ceremonial of Bishops*. This special permission would usually be given during feasts of great solemnity, such as Christmas, Easter, Pentecost, and the like.

> 16. Since the singing must always be the chief thing, the organ and the instruments may only sustain and never crush it.[24]

This is self-explanatory, and is chiefly aimed at instrumentalists who would play as though their instruments were more important than the choir. This abuse would most often be done with too much volume, disrespecting the balance between singers and instrumentalists.

> 17. It is not lawful to introduce the singing with long preludes, or to interrupt it with intermezzi.[25]

A common practice in sacred music of the nineteenth century was to introduce major compositions with long preludes, usually with various instruments. These preludes were often long-winded, and lengthened the liturgy to an intolerable degree. This would also happen when the main composition would be interrupted with an *intermezzo*, which could be either vocal or instrumental. Pius was right to proscribe these practices, which might work well in a concert or operatic venue, but not in church.

> 18. The music of the organ in the accompaniment, preludes, interludes, and so on must be played not only according to the proper

---

[24] PLSM 229.
[25] PLSM 229.

character of the instrument, but also according to all the rules of real sacred music, which have been described above.[26]

These regulations (no. 18) are intended to safeguard the integrity of sacred organ music, which music can be used to accompany singers and other instruments or be played solo at various points in the liturgy. The organ, with its many stops, can produce a very wide range of volume and many combinations of sounds. Some of these combinations could be used to excess, and thus be out of character for the liturgy. Hence, the organist must respect the three qualities of sacred music in the choice and performance of organ compositions during the liturgy.

> 19. The use of the piano-forte is forbidden in churches, as also that of all noisy or irreverent instruments such as drums, kettledrums, cymbals, triangles and so on.[27]

The prohibition of the piano is because it has primarily developed as a secular instrument, and thus accumulated a secular repertoire. Because of this secular repertoire, and even when it is used to play a sacred composition, say

---

[26] PLSM 229.

[27] PLSM 229. In the nineteenth century, the piano was often referred to as the "pianoforte" because this was the name of the instrument when it first appeared in the year 1700, designed by Bartolomeo Cristofori. (At one point in history, it was also known as the "fortepiano.") The designation reflects the fact that the "pianoforte" can produce sounds that are "piano" (the Italian word for "soft"), as well as sounds that are "forte" (the Italian word for "loud"). It also implies that the piano can achieve a wide range of dynamics – from very soft to very loud. Pius simply used the designation that was more common in the late nineteenth century. Later, as the twentieth century progresses, the "forte" is gradually dropped, and the word "piano" eventually becomes universally used to signify the instrument. For more on the prohibition of piano, guitar, and other secular instruments, see Kwasniewski, *Good Music*, 234-44.

a transcription of a motet, hymn, or Mass, the instrument has too many secular connotations for use in church.

Although Pius does not state it specifically, the same principle applies to the guitar, since it too is primarily a secular instrument with a largely secular repertoire. Moreover, all one need do is attend the typical *Novus Ordo Missae* to see why both the piano and the guitar should never be used in the liturgy of the Catholic Church.

Pius also specifically prohibits "drums," "kettledrums," "cymbals," "triangles," and the like. These are all included in the category of percussion instruments, and are typically used in modern symphony orchestras. They also have a primarily secular use, particularly in the secular orchestral music repertory.

> 20. Bands are strictly forbidden to play in church, and only for some special reason, after the consent of the Bishop has been obtained, may a certain number of specially-chosen wind instruments be allowed, which must be carefully selected and suitable to their object; and the music they play must always be reverent, appropriate, and in every way like that of the organ.
>
> 21. Bands may be allowed by the Bishop in processions outside the church, as long as they do not perform secular music. The best plan on such occasions would be for the band only to accompany some hymn or sacred chant, either in Latin or in the vulgar tongue, sung by the choir or by the members of the confraternities that take part in the procession.[28]

As is clear from this paragraph (no. 20), bands, as such, are prohibited for use in the liturgy. The concept of a band for Pius is the typical European "band" that consists of woodwind instruments such as the flute, clarinet,

---

[28] PLSM 229.

oboe, and bassoon, as well as the common brass instruments, such as the French horn, trumpet, trombone, and tuba. (Pius is obviously not referring to such things as "pop," "swing," or "rock" bands.) European bands were quite common in the Italy of Pius's day in church settings, for ceremonial processionals outside of church, and for general entertainment. For Pius, however, these bands and their "popular" music were all too secular-sounding for use during the sacred liturgy, and therefore had to be prohibited.

Pius goes on to state that for special occasions, and always with permission of the local bishop, certain wind instruments may be allowed for use in the liturgy. Pius does not state specifically which instruments would be allowed, but he provides us with a few basic principles for the selection process: the instruments chosen must be suitable to their objects, always be reverent and appropriate, and "in every way like that of the organ." What this last phrase really means is that the instruments in question should produce a sound that resembles the sustaining qualities of the organ, as well as the typical timbres of the pipe organ as heard in the Catholic liturgy. These instruments should also produce music that is reverent, and that always respects the three qualities of sacred music.

In paragraph no. 21, Pius allows the use of bands for processions *outside* of the church building to continue, as long as the musicians have permission from the local bishop, and do not perform any kind of secular music. Pius then gives his recommendation for the best way to use the band, which would be to accompany some hymn or spiritual song (*"cantico spirituale"*), either in Latin or in the vernacular, which would then be sung by the choir, or by members of the confraternities that participate in the procession.

THE LENGTH OF LITURGICAL MUSIC

22. It is not lawful to make the priest at the altar wait longer than the ceremonies allow, for the sake of the singing or instrumental music. According to the laws of the Church, the Sanctus of the Mass must be finished before the elevation; wherefore in this point the celebrant must attend to the singers. The Gloria and the Credo, according to Gregorian tradition, should be comparatively short.[29]

This passage is mostly very clear. The only part that seems ambiguous is the clause: "wherefore in this point the celebrant must attend to the singers." This last statement is clarified by its parallel passage in the *Votum* of 1893, where one finds the following:

In regard to this point the celebrant must have fitting regard for the singers.[30]

Pius means here that the celebrant must also have a certain respect for the task that the singers are trying to accomplish. Thus, for example, if the celebrant tends to be fast, he should slow his own reading of the texts of the Canon so as not to finish too soon, thus making it appear that he is waiting for the choir to finish. The choir singers, on the other hand, with due regard for the celebrant, should make sure that they are finished with the Sanctus before the elevation.[31] In other words, there ought to be careful coordination between the celebrant and the choir.

---

[29] PLSM 229-230.
[30] *Votum* of 1893 in PLSM 229-230.
[31] Recall that, at the time Pius X is writing, it was customary to view the *Sanctus* and *Benedictus* as separate movements (a practice that has its roots in the Renaissance polyphonic Masses), and to sing the *Benedictus* after the consecrations. Thus, when he says that the *Sanctus* should be finished before the consecration, he is not including the *Benedictus* in this assessment.

> 23. As a general principle it is a very grave abuse, and one to be altogether condemned, to make the liturgy of sacred functions appear a secondary matter, and, as it were, the servant of the music. On the contrary, the music is really only a part of the liturgy and its humble attendant.[32]

This passage is aimed directly at the pride of *"prima donna"* musicians. These musicians would dare to think that music is more important than the liturgy; still worse, they would conduct a service in which it appears that the liturgy is a "secondary matter," that is, less important than the music. Pius scorns this attitude by stating that in practice this is a "very grave abuse." It should also be noted that there is a delicate balance between sacred music and the liturgy, which is very easily upset by too much music, too many solos, loud and noisy instruments, and vocal "grandstanding."

Pius then reaffirms the Church's true teaching by stating the real place of sacred music, namely, that it is only a *part* of the liturgy and its humble servant. Sacred music exists to *serve* the liturgy, not the other way around. However, this last statement should not be construed to mean that sacred music is unimportant, or that it would be a greater sign of humility to minimize, or, God forbid, do away with sacred music altogether. To counter this unreasonable attitude, recall that Pius states that sacred music is an *"integral part"* of the liturgy. Thus, sacred music is an *essential* and therefore a very important part of the sung liturgy – but never more important than the liturgy itself.

THE CHIEF MEANS OF PROCURING GOOD SACRED MUSIC

We now come to the penultimate section of the motu proprio, which articulates the best ways to achieve the

---

[32] MP in PLSM 230.

goals of Catholic sacred music. In many respects, this section provides the basis for the implementation of the reform, and alludes to the institutions of the Church that would be involved in that implementation. As we will see later, these rules point to major Church institutions that will be necessary for the reform.

> 24. In order that these instructions be exactly carried out, the Bishops should, if they have not already done so, appoint in each Diocese a special commission of persons who are really competent in the matter, to whom they will entrust the duty of watching over the music performed in the churches in whatever way may seem most advisable. The commission will insist on the music being not only good in itself, but also proportionate to the capacity of the singers, so that it may always be well executed. [33]

In paragraph no. 24, Pius begins by stating that in order for these instructions to be carried out "exactly," bishops are to establish in their diocese "a special commission" (*"una Commissione speciale"*) of persons who are "truly competent" (*"veramente competenti"*) in matters of sacred music. The members of the commission will be charged with overseeing the music performed in the various churches of the diocese. Notice that these members are to be "truly competent," not musical amateurs, not musical "buffs" or "aficionados" whose musical education might consist of a mere "music appreciation" course; rather, they are to be truly qualified and thoroughly trained musicians.

The task of this commission will consist of making sure that the music is not only "good in itself" (*"per se buone"*), but also "proportionate to the capacity of the singers," so that the music will "always be well executed" (*"sempre bene eseguite"*). These passages clearly hark back to (and are

---

[33] PLSM 230.

corollaries of) the principle that all sacred music must *thoroughly* and *completely* possess *the sense of the sacred*, both in itself *and* in the way it is performed. This means that if a choir can sing Gregorian chant well but is not able to render classical polyphony in an acceptable way, that group should not perform classical polyphony during the liturgy. Fundamentally then, if a composition cannot be well executed, *it should not be done.*

> 25. In ecclesiastical seminaries and institutions the traditional Gregorian chant recommended above must be studied with all diligence and love, according to the law of the Council of Trent; and superiors should be generous in their appreciation and encouragement of this point with their students.
>
> In the same way the formation of a school of singing for the execution of figured music of a right and liturgical kind should be encouraged among the students wherever it is possible.[34]

In paragraph no. 25, Pius is giving priority to the study of Gregorian chant, particularly for seminarians. This makes perfect sense since in the sung liturgy (i.e., "High Masses") there will always be sacred music, because a "sung liturgy," by definition, must have liturgical music. Since the chant has priority of place, and is the only music that can be sung in certain parts of the Mass and Divine Office, it is logical to give priority, in priestly formation, to the Gregorian chant. Pius also mentions "institutions," that is, music schools, as it is also important for those laymen who will participate in the liturgy to have a good grasp of the chant as well. Later, we will see that the study of Gregorian chant in the seminaries also includes such things as vocal instruction, music theory, music history, and general musicianship, among others.

---

[34] PLSM 230.

Pius also mentions the law of the Council of Trent, which articulates the traditional liturgical law underpinning his position.

Pius hardly needed to stress that superiors should be "generous" in their appreciation and encouragement of the learning of Gregorian chant. For what ecclesiastic would, in his right mind, discourage such a noble thing—unless, of course, he is an enemy of the Church.

In the second paragraph of no. 25, Pius also underscores the importance, for seminarians, of the study of good and correct sacred polyphonic music (what Pius calls "figured music"). This study should also be encouraged among seminarians so that they have a proper appreciation for sacred polyphony, especially classical polyphony.

This again illustrates Pius's intelligent and balanced approach to the sacred music of the Church. He is neither encouraging the elimination of sacred polyphony for an all-Gregorian chant sung liturgy, nor is he supporting the de-emphasis of the chant for the promotion of sacred polyphony, even the highly sophisticated classical polyphony. Rather, he is advocating in a gentle way that the sung liturgy should normally have *both* chant and polyphony. Now I stress the word "should," because Pius does say that one *can* have a liturgy with chant alone, and that this does not mean that the liturgy is "less solemn" than one with both chant and polyphony. However, as a practical matter, because both in our time and in Pius's time we live in a society in which polyphonic music abounds, congregations will be more familiar with polyphonic style music than the monophonic style of chant. In addition, the most important reason is that there is an abundance of extraordinarily beautiful polyphonic sacred music that complements the great beauty of the Gregorian chant, which, when heard together in a liturgy, adds a sublime variety that simply cannot be surpassed.

26. In the usual lectures on liturgy, moral theology, and canon law, which are given to students of theology, the points which specially touch the principles and laws of sacred music must also be duly explained, and means should be sought to complete this teaching with some special instruction on the aesthetics of sacred art, so that the clerics may not leave the seminary without having right ideas on these subjects, which are also part of ecclesiastical knowledge.[35]

In this paragraph (no. 26), Pius emphasizes the importance of imparting to seminarians an understanding of the laws of sacred music. Courses on sacred music are to be considered an essential component of the standard seminary curriculum. Included in these courses on sacred music should also be "special instruction" on the aesthetics of sacred art. Aesthetics is a branch of philosophy that studies the "beautiful," that is, it examines questions related to the human experience of, and responses to, beauty in all of the fine arts, including music. Knowledge of the aesthetics of sacred art is crucial to understanding why Catholic sacred music is the highest music one can compose or perform. It also gives astute insights into why some art is bad and evil, and why some kinds of music, such as "rock 'n' roll," are truly antithetical to Catholic sacred music. Pius insists on this knowledge so that future clerics will have correct ideas on these topics, which are also an important part of ecclesiastical knowledge.

27. Care must be taken to restore, at least in connection with the more important churches, the ancient choir schools which have already been introduced again with very good results in many places. Indeed it would not be difficult for zealous priests to establish such schools

---

[35] PLSM 230.

even in small parishes and in the country, and they would form an easy means of gathering together both children and grown-up people to their profit and the edification of all the parish.[36]

Paragraph no. 27 stresses the importance of the restoration of the "ancient choir schools," which had already been introduced in the nineteenth century with positive results. These "choir schools" are traditionally known as *Scholae Cantorum*. A *Schola Cantorum* was a choir run by a choirmaster, usually a well-known composer and singer, who, in the employ of the Church, provided the Gregorian chant and polyphonic sacred music for the liturgy. In the early Church, a *Schola* was made up entirely of men. Later, as four-part classical polyphony developed, it was found expedient to use boys on the alto and soprano parts, while retaining men on the tenor and bass parts.

With the introduction of boys into the *Scholae*, the responsibilities for vocal and musical training fell to the choirmaster, who was obliged to train the boys in voice, the fundamentals of music, the solfège system, music theory, Gregorian chant, and the like. By the fourteenth century, many church musicians received their initial training in a *Schola Cantorum*.

Although Pius desires the establishment of *Scholae* in the "more important churches," nevertheless, he also hopes that these schools will be established even in churches located in "small parishes and in the country." This passage should disprove all arguments that Pius intended his legislation to apply primarily to large, famous churches, or only to parishes in major cities. Actually, Pius wanted *every* Roman Rite Catholic Church in the world to echo with the magnificent sounds of Gregorian chant and sacred polyphony.

---

[36] PLSM 231.

28. All higher schools of Church music should be kept up and encouraged in every way where they already exist, and as far as possible new ones should be founded. It is most important that the Church should herself provide instruction for her own choirmasters, organists, and singers, so that she may inspire them with the right principles of this sacred art.[37]

This paragraph makes it clear that Pius wanted the Church not only to maintain the already functioning Church-sponsored music schools, but also to found new music schools for the instruction and development of the Church's future musicians. An examination of the various *curricula* of the many Church-sponsored music schools makes it very evident that Pius intended these schools to procure well-trained musicians for the performance and composition of true Catholic sacred music. Later in this book, we will explore the rich and complex *curricula* of the many levels of sacred music instruction that Pius intended for the Church.

CONCLUSION

29. Finally, we desire all choirmasters, singers, and clerics, all superiors of seminaries, ecclesiastical institutions, and religious communities, all parish priests and rectors of churches, all canons of collegiate and cathedral churches, and, most especially, the Ordinaries of all Dioceses, zealously to support these wise reforms, which have been long desired and unanimously hoped for by all, in order that no injury be done to the authority of the Church, which has already often proposed them and now insists on them once more.

Given at Our Apostolic Palace of the Vatican, on the feast of the Virgin Martyr Saint Cecilia,

---

[37] PLSM 231.

November 22, 1903, in the first year of Our
Pontificate.[38]

In paragraph no. 29, Pius concludes his famous motu
proprio with an exhortation to a wide variety of Church
institutions to support "zealously" these excellent reforms.
The above list of the many Church institutions partici-
pating in the implementation process is truly impressive;
it also gives us a clear indication of how extensive Pius
intends the reform to be.

In the last lines of the first paragraph of no. 29, Pius
pleads for the cooperation and support of all those
involved in the reform, so that the authority of the
Church will not be undermined in this endeavor. Later,
we will survey the role of these various institutions when
the implementation phase of the reform is examined.

This concludes the commentary on the principles of
Catholic sacred music as articulated in the motu proprio
of 1903. At this point, it is important to note that not
every possible aspect of the principles contained in the
motu proprio of 1903 has been examined. Nevertheless,
most of the major issues contained therein have been
explicated. It should also be remembered that one could
take almost any paragraph in the motu proprio and easily write an essay on that paragraph alone – such is the
richness and depth of Pius's thought.

---

[38] PLSM 231.

PART II

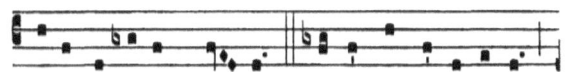

Canonical, Historical, and Practical Aspects

CHAPTER 4
Canonical Considerations

WE TURN NOW TO A STUDY OF SOME OF the canonical implications of the motu proprio of 1903. There are four key issues in this discussion of canonical aspects: first, the canonical status of the motu proprio of 1903 at the time of its promulgation; second, the canonical status from the death of Pius X up to the beginning of Vatican II;[1] third, the canonical status from the time of Vatican II to the promulgation of the new *Code of Canon Law* in 1983; and fourth, the current canonical status of this document. Before beginning to answer these questions, however, some preliminary remarks are in order.

PRELIMINARIES

Whenever a body of laws is issued, it is important to distinguish between the mind of the legislator and the actual expression of the laws in the official legislation itself. It is also incumbent on the intended subjects to determine the binding power of the laws, as well as any punitive sanctions attached to the violation of those laws. This applies to any law, be it civil or ecclesiastical. These considerations are of paramount importance, particularly with the motu proprio of 1903, because even after the promulgation of the document, there are those who try to undermine the reform by claiming that the motu

---

[1] The dates for Vatican II are October 11, 1962 to December 8, 1965.

proprio is not truly binding on all Catholic musicians. Their arguments are fundamentally that the legislation in the motu proprio merely contains suggestions and recommendations, and that one need not follow the laws if he disagrees. In other words, they are implying that Pius's sacred music legislation is only *directive* in nature.

Now the discipline of Roman Catholic canon law is a highly specialized subject, requiring proper credentials from accredited Church institutions and many years of intensive study. I do not possess these credentials. Thus, I am not able, of myself, to render an expert canon law opinion on this topic. Nevertheless, we can still examine these questions in light of the opinions of respected scholars on this subject.[2]

---

[2] One such respected sacred music scholar who has rendered an opinion on this subject is Robert F. Hayburn, author of *Papal Legislation on Sacred Music 95 AD to 1977 AD*. Father Hayburn was a leading sacred music scholar who contributed much to the promotion of Catholic sacred music, especially an understanding of the law before Vatican II. His excellent study on sacred music contains a section on canon law aspects of Pius X's sacred music legislation, with special focus on the motu proprio of 1903. This section is entitled: "Binding Force of Papal Documents on Sacred Music." His understanding of the legal status of the motu proprio before Vatican II accords quite well with Pius's legislative intent. Unfortunately, though, even Fr. Hayburn appears to have been deceived by the façade of traditionalism in the Conciliar and post-Conciliar documents, since he apparently, at the time he wrote his text (late 1970s), considered the Conciliar document on the liturgy, *Sacrosanctum Concilium*, as well as Pope Paul VI's 1967 Instruction *Musicam Sacram*, to be consistent with the reform of Pius X. (See also my comment in footnote 28 below.) Also note that Fr. Hayburn's text was written before the 1983 *Code of Canon Law* was promulgated.

Another scholar is Florentius Romita, who has written on the subject of liturgical law and sacred music. See Florentius Romita, *Jus musicae liturgicae* (Rome: Edizione Liturgicae, 1947).

Regarding the canonical status of sacred music laws in the post-Conciliar era, numerous studies have been done demonstrating the insertion of legislative loopholes used by neo-Modernists to undercut the traditional legislation on sacred music and the liturgy of the Church.

THE STATUS OF THE MOTU PROPRIO:
ITS PROMULGATION TO THE DEATH OF PIUS X

In our quest to answer the first question, it is important to distinguish two categories of law: *preceptive* and *directive*. According to Fr. Hayburn, *preceptive* laws are those requiring *strict obedience*. *Directive* laws, on the other hand, do not require strict obedience, but are merely suggestive.

> A preceptive law contains strict orders which must be obeyed. It sets down a principle which must be followed in conscience and is not a matter of whim or caprice. For example, the Friday abstinence law forbade meat on that day.
>
> A directive law contains recommendations to the faithful. For example, Pope Leo XIII recommended that all Catholics spend at least fifteen minutes each day in reading Sacred Scripture. However, one is not bound to spend this time daily in Bible reading. In other words, his directive law does not bind in conscience; rather it is a recommendation or invitation.[3]

The next issue concerns the *binding force* of papal legislation on Church music. In order to address this problem, we must turn to the law current at the time of the motu proprio of 1903. Now the first code of canon law would not be issued until 1917, when Benedict XV promulgated the *Code of Canon Law*. This codification of Church law is largely the work of Pope Saint Pius X, but was not promulgated until three years after Pius X's death. Yet even though this Code came out in 1917, it truly reflected Catholic Church law current at the time the motu proprio of 1903 is issued. It is perfectly valid then to consider the canonical status of the motu proprio, at the time of its promulgation, in light of the 1917 *Code of Canon Law*.

---

[3] PLSM 513.

Fr. Hayburn cites three canons from this Code that are important for answering the aforesaid question: Canons 18, 49, and 1264. Canon 18 states: "Ecclesiastical laws must be interpreted according to the proper meaning of the terms of the laws considered in their context."[4] Here again is the word *context*, which, as mentioned previously (pp. 46–49), must be considered in order to interpret ecclesiastical documents properly. This means that one must consider all relevant contexts, such as historical, canonical, theological, and the like.

Canon 49 reads: "Rescripts must be understood according to the proper meaning of their words and the common usage of the language, and must not be extended to other cases besides those expressly mentioned."[5] Rescripts are responses to questions given to a legitimate Church authority. They could be issued in the form of bulls, briefs, apostolic letters, or simple rescripts. Note well the emphasis on considering the proper meaning of the words, and the common usage of the language in the rescript. Moreover, note that rescripts only apply to those cases mentioned explicitly in the rescript, and cannot be extended to others.

Canon 1264 reiterates an important precept from the Council of Trent, and then includes a crucial statement on the general nature of liturgical laws governing sacred music: "All music, whether instrumental or vocal, which contains anything lascivious or impure, must be entirely kept out of churches. The liturgical laws concerning sacred music shall be observed."[6] This last statement indicates that liturgical laws on sacred music have the *same force and binding power* as any other liturgical law of the Church.

In order to determine the *binding power* of a law (that is, whether a law is preceptive or directive) one must

---

[4] 1917 *Code of Canon Law* in PLSM 513–514.
[5] PLSM 514.
[6] PLSM 515.

examine the *exact wording* of the document. According to Fr. Hayburn:

> Directive rubrics or regulations are easily distinguished from those that are preceptive. Directive enactments are generally couched in such terms as: "It is praiseworthy," "we recommend," "it is a salutary practice," etc. However, preceptive regulations are definitely given in such terms as: "It is to be observed," "so we write anew and command observance," "the custom is to be eliminated," "all custom to the contrary notwithstanding," etc.[7]

By way of illustration, Fr. Hayburn cites a decree, written in the form of a question and answer, from the Congregation of Sacred Rites: *Briocen*, no. 3069, of August 14, 1858 that contains directive laws concerning the use of Gregorian chant at Rogation Masses. The directive nature of the law is clearly indicated by the last phrase "it is not strictly commanded":

> In churches in which there are many priests, must not this Rogation Mass altogether be celebrated with chant, or does it suffice to celebrate this Mass without chant, when the Procession has taken place?
>
> Answer to question three: It is more appropriate, according to the rubrics, that the Mass be sung; however, it is not strictly commanded....[8]

An example of a document containing one of the earliest instances of preceptive legislation on sacred music is *Una res*, issued by Pope Leo IV (847–855) to Abbot Honoratus:

> Therefore, We command under sentence of excommunication that, in the singing and

---

[7] PLSM 514.
[8] Congregation of Sacred Rites in PLSM 441.

readings of your churches, you carry them out in no other way than that which Pope St. Gregory handed down and We hold, that you cultivate and sing this tradition always and with all your powers. For if, which We hardly believe, anyone should try, now or in the future, in any way whatever, to lead you back or turn you aside to any other tradition beside the one which We gave to you, We not only command that he be excommunicated from the holy body and blood of Our Lord Jesus Christ, but We declare by Our authority and also the authority of all Our predecessors that he shall remain in perpetual anathema for his presumptuous audacity.[9]

It does not take a doctoral degree in canon law to grasp the preceptive nature of this document. Incidentally, please note the fierce determination on the part of Pope Leo IV to *preserve* liturgical tradition – a refreshing contrast to the rubbish found in many post-Conciliar documents.

With these preliminaries established, we are ready to examine the binding force of the motu proprio of 1903. In the last paragraph of the "Introduction," Pius X indicates the binding nature of his legislation:

Wherefore, in order that no one may in the future put forward as an excuse that he does not rightly know his duty, in order that all possible uncertainty concerning laws already made may be removed, We consider it advisable to sum up shortly the principles that govern the sacred music of liturgical services, and to present again the chief laws of the Church against faults in this matter. And therefore We publish this Our Instruction *motu proprio et ex certa scientia* [on our own accord and from certain knowledge], and We desire with all the authority of Our apostolic office that it have the force of law as a

---

[9] Pope Leo IV, *Una Res* in PLSM 514.

> canonical code concerning sacred music, and We
> impose upon all by Our own signature the duty
> of the most exact obedience to it.[10]

Here the preceptive nature of Pius X's intentions is unmistakable, particularly when he states, "We impose upon all by Our own signature the duty of the most exact obedience to it." If Pius did not intend his legislation to be preceptive, why would he use such strong wording? He obviously uses such language because he *does* intend for these laws to be obeyed scrupulously by all Catholic musicians.

After establishing the preceptive (and thus binding) nature of the legislation in the motu proprio of 1903, Fr. Hayburn next raises the logical question of whether these preceptive laws *bind in conscience*. In other words, does Pius X's legislation bind under *pain of sin*?

According to Fr. Hayburn, three conditions must be established before a law *binds in conscience*: "1) It must be solemnly promulgated, 2) Experts in the field must concur that it binds, 3) There are usually grave sanctions for the persons who break the law."[11]

The first condition, solemn promulgation, is satisfied by a document's inclusion in the publications of the *Acta Apostolicae Sedis*, the official organ of the Church. The motu proprio of 1903 is not only included in the *Acta*, it is also reinforced by a second decree issued from the Sacred Congregation of Rites on January 8, 1904: "The same Most Holy Lord (Pius X) by means of this Sacred Congregation commands and ordains that the said Instruction be received by all the Churches and observed in a holy manner..."[12]

---

[10] MP in PLSM 514.
[11] PLSM 516.
[12] Congregation of Sacred Rites in PLSM 517.

Regarding the second condition, moral theologians base the moral obligation to obey a preceptive positive ecclesiastical law on three things: first, on the will and intention of the lawgiver; second, on the gravity of the matter; and third, on the proportion that exists between the object of the law and the means prescribed to attain it. The will and intention of the lawgiver should be evident in the language of the document. In the motu proprio of 1903, this is blatantly obvious.

Regarding the gravity of the matter, at the very outset of his document Pius gives us a superb description of the grave responsibilities of the pastoral office in preserving and safeguarding the liturgy of the Church. This opening paragraph is worth quoting again:

> One of the chief duties of the pastoral office, not only in this Holy See which We, although unworthy, by the inscrutable decree of Providence occupy, but in every diocese of the Church, is certainly to maintain and increase the beauty of the house of God, in which the holy mysteries of our faith are celebrated, in which the Christian people come together to receive the grace of the Sacraments, and to assist at the Holy Sacrifice of the Altar, to adore the Blessed Sacrament, and to join in the public and solemn liturgical prayers of the Church. Nothing then should be allowed in the sacred building that could disturb or lessen the piety and devotion of the faithful, nothing that could be a reasonable motive for displeasure or scandal, nothing especially that could offend against the dignity and holiness of the sacred rites, and that would therefore be unworthy of the house of prayer, or of the majesty of Almighty God.[13]

Moreover, it only requires a brief look at the myriad

---

[13] MP in PLSM 222.

problems in the *Novus Ordo Missae*, and the resulting evil consequences of tampering with the Mass, to see just how grave a responsibility the pope has in safeguarding that treasure. Msgr. Florentius Romita remarks on the gravity of the matter regarding liturgical *praxis*:

> The seriousness (gravity) of the obligation of the laws depends primarily on the seriousness of the matter, secondly on the will of the superior, and finally from the seriousness of the penalties whether special or general. As to the matter there can be no doubt; for, whatever pertains to Divine Worship has always been considered grave matter, and the solemn will and intention of the Superior is made clear from the tenor of the laws.[14]

Since the motu proprio of 1903 is directly concerned with sacred music used in Divine Worship, it is deeply involved in a very grave matter.

Regarding the third requirement for expert concurrence on the binding nature of a document, namely, the proportion that exists between the object of the law and the means prescribed to attain it, it is clear that the means are proportionate to the end. In this regard, Pius gives us many regulations and advice that, if followed correctly, will bring about the desired end, which is the correct use of Catholic sacred music. Furthermore, recall that Pius even includes a section in the motu proprio of 1903 on how best to procure sacred music.

The third condition for establishing that a law binds in conscience – that there usually are grave sanctions for the persons who break the law – is exemplified in past legislation on sacred music. For example, the legislation of Leo IV quoted earlier contains the grave penalty

---

[14] Romita, *Jus musicae liturgicae*, quoted in PLSM 517.

of excommunication for disobedience. The 1917 *Code of Canon Law*, however, contains no explicit penalties for disobeying musical regulations. In the motu proprio of 1903 there are also no explicit sanctions for noncompliance with these musical laws. Yet according to Florentius Romita, this absence of penalties does not mitigate the force of these laws. This is because the absence of penalties is compensated for by the dismissal of disobedient church musicians from their posts as singers, organists, and choirmasters.[15] In Pius's reform, this is primarily to be done by diocesan commissions, which are set up to ensure that proper standards are enforced. Hence, at the time of promulgation, the effect is the same, and there truly are punitive sanctions in place against insolent musicians.

Thus, we can conclude that Church music laws, as expressed in the motu proprio of 1903 at the time of promulgation, are mostly *preceptive*, and require *true obedience* from individual church musicians. Fr. Hayburn sums this up concisely:

> Church music laws are, therefore, for the most part preceptive. Such commands call for an active obedience from the individual's inner spirit. By his acquiescence he makes an external manifestation of his internal assent of the will to the authority of God's Church.[16]

Concerning those who do not comply with this legislation, Fr. Hayburn notes that there seem to be three principal categories of church musicians who fail to obey the regulations: first, those who are ignorant of the law itself; second, those who know the law but interpret it to be merely directive in nature; and third, those who know the law, know that the law is binding in conscience,

---

[15] PLSM 517.
[16] PLSM 518.

and yet refuse to obey. These last are the worst because they prefer their own personal expression, or to "show off" their musical talents. The first two causes can be remedied by proper education. The third, however, is much more difficult to amend.[17]

Yet Pius believed that most musicians, once they understood the reasonableness of his legislation, would comply despite penalties for disobedience, because they would be able to understand the good fruits that compliance with the law would engender for the Church.

THE CANONICAL STATUS OF THE MOTU PROPRIO: THE DEATH OF PIUS X TO VATICAN II

Concerning the second issue, the period following the death of Pope St. Pius X to the dawn of the Second Vatican Council is one of overall growth, development, and further implementation of the principles of sacred music as formulated in the motu proprio of 1903. A succession of three popes, namely, Benedict XV, Pius XI, and

---

[17] PLSM 516. Some have tried to argue that because *Tra le Sollecitudini* of 1903 is written in the form of a motu proprio, the legislation contained therein, for that reason, is merely directive. The reason cited is a description given of the motu proprio by noted canonist Amleto Cardinal Cicognani in *Canon Law* (Westminster, MD: Newman Press, 1949), 81, which states: "Motu proprios, or papal documents issued with the clause motu proprio, are given by the Pope of his own accord, in the form of a simple decree. They are never issued in the solemn form of a Bull or of a Brief, and deal with matters of no special moment, in particular with administrative negotiations" (PLSM 507). However, if we remember Pius X's clear legislative intent, why would he use a type of document that would undercut his own legislation? Obviously (using common sense), at least in this case, the type of document does not affect the binding nature of the legislation contained in it. Furthermore, Fr. Hayburn gives the motu proprio of 1903 itself as an example of a famous motu proprio, and one that contains *preceptive* regulations. Why would Fr. Hayburn say this if the type of document nullified the preceptive nature of the legislation contained therein? Thus, this objection is patently absurd.

Pius XII, all significantly aided the growth and development of the reform.[18]

In terms of canon law, Pope Benedict XV continued to implement and develop the reform in strict conformity to Pope St. Pius X's designs. This is evident in his ardent and enthusiastic support of the great Pontifical Institute of Sacred Music, which was founded by Pius X himself to promote the highest standards of Catholic sacred music. Many examples of Benedict's adherence to the reforms of Pius X can also be found in the Apostolic Constitution for the Choral Chaplain Singers of the Liberian Basilica. One brief example from this constitution shows that Benedict understands the importance of chant being "performed carefully and correctly" according to the principles of Pius's motu proprio of 1903: "and also they have made efforts to see that the Gregorian chant, which has been restored to its pristine purity, might be performed carefully and correctly, according to the norms which Our Predecessor of Holy Memory, Pius X, prescribed, in his motu proprio of November 22, 1903."[19]

The next pope, Pius XI, also continued to promote the growth of the reform with his monumental *Divini Cultus Sanctitatem* of December 20, 1928. Fr. Hayburn emphasizes the fact that Pius XI's great apostolic constitution is partly written to reassert the preceptive nature of Pius X's motu proprio of 1903:

> Written to reemphasize the preceptive character of *Tra le sollecitudini*, it restates the principles of the earlier work and makes more specific certain points in it. It is concerned with the fuller

---

[18] There will be a discussion of the way that these popes contributed to the implementation of the reform later in this book: see chapter 5.
[19] Pope Benedict XV, *Apostolic Constitution for the Choral Chapel Singers of the Liberian Basilica* in PLSM 320.

participation of the faithful in the worship of the Church, following the suggestions of Pius X, and the more exact rules for teaching sacred music in seminaries.[20]

Pius XI stresses the preceptive nature of the regulations in *Divini Cultus Sanctitatem* with these words, which by implication defend the preceptive character of Pius X's legislation:

> It is, however, to be deplored that these most wise laws in some places have not been fully observed, and therefore their intended results have not obtained. We know that some have declared that these laws, though so solemnly promulgated, were not binding upon their obedience.... These things We command, declare and sanction, decreeing that this Apostolic Constitution be now and in future firm, valid, and efficacious, that it obtain full and complete effect, all things to the contrary notwithstanding. Let no man, therefore, infringe this Constitution by Us promulgated, nor dare to contravene it.[21]

The third pre-Conciliar pope, Pius XII, also, for the most part, continued to promote the growth and development of Pius's reform. I say "for the most part" because there are several regulations that seem to deviate from Pius X's legislation, particularly in the last major document on sacred music to come from the reign of Pius XII, the *Instruction* of 1958.[22]

---

[20] PLSM 327.

[21] Pope Pius XI, *Divini Cultus Sanctitatem* in PLSM 515.

[22] The *Instruction* of 1958 was written by sacred music experts and members of the Pontifical Commission for the general renovation of the liturgy. It was issued on September 3, 1958 by the Prefect of the Sacred Congregation of Rites with the explicit approval of Pope Pius XII. I will address some of the problems with this document later in this book.

Besides the *Instruction* of 1958, the most significant documents on sacred music written by Pius XII himself are *Mediator Dei* and *Musicae Sacrae Disciplina. Mediator Dei* is primarily concerned with the liturgy as a whole. Nevertheless, there are several important paragraphs on sacred music. Nos. 187 and 191 demonstrate the preceptive nature of the content of *Mediator Dei* as a whole, as well as those paragraphs that focus on sacred music:

> 187. First of all, you must strive that with due reverence and faith all obey the decrees of the Council of Trent, of the Roman Pontiffs, and of the Congregation of Sacred Rites, and what the liturgical books ordain concerning external public worship.
>
> 191. As regards music, let the clear and guiding norms of the Apostolic See be scrupulously observed.[23]

The most significant document concerned exclusively with sacred music to come *directly* from Pius XII is the encyclical *Musicae Sacrae Disciplina*, which was promulgated on December 25, 1955. This encyclical continues to follow the principles established by Pius X. The document does allow, however, some latitude in the use of orchestral instruments and in the use of some religious compositions at non-liturgical services. Pius XII alludes to the preceptive nature of sacred music laws, as well as adaptations to certain "contemporary conditions," in the following paragraph:

> 3. We hope, therefore, that what St. Pius X rightly decreed in the document which he accurately called the "legal code of sacred music" (Motu proprio, *Tra le sollecitudini dell'ufficio pastorale, Acta Pii X*, 1:77) may be confirmed and inculcated anew, shown in a new light and

---

[23] Pope Pius XII, *Mediator Dei* in PLSM 340.

strengthened by new proofs. We hope that the
noble art of sacred music – adapted to contemporary conditions and in some way enriched – may
ever more perfectly accomplish its mission. [24]

Thus, with perhaps several exceptions in the *Instruction* of 1958, the sacred music laws contained in the motu
proprio of 1903 remained largely intact and protected by
pre-Conciliar Popes.

CANONICAL STATUS OF THE MOTU PROPRIO: VATICAN II TO THE 1983 *CODE OF CANON LAW*

Concerning the third issue, when looking back over
the last sixty years, the answer to the question of the
canonical status of the motu proprio of 1903, from the
time of the Second Vatican Council to 1983, seems to be
one of "official" obrogation. Obrogation occurs when new
legislation is intended to replace existing laws, but the
documents do not contain specific words that formally
abolish these existing laws. (The use of specific words
to indicate that a law has been abolished is known in
canon law as "abrogation.") This obrogation appears to
have happened because even before the end of Vatican
II, a *de facto* suppression of traditional Catholic sacred
music was in effect. [25] The suppression was quietly "legalized" after the close of the Council, then supported by
legislation contained in both Conciliar and post-Conciliar

---

[24] Pope Pius XII, *Musicae Sacrae Disciplina* in PLSM 346.

[25] In my second year as an altar boy, in 1964, I witnessed the
beginning of the destruction of the liturgy in my home parish
of Nativity of Our Lord in St. Paul, Minnesota. Some of these
changes consisted in the use of guitars and popular style music
in the liturgy, the priest facing the people at an ugly new "table,"
the absence of the prayers at the foot of the altar, the omission of
the Last Gospel, and changes in the use of the bells, to name just a
few. Please note that in 1964, the Second Vatican Council was still
in session, and would not end until December 8, 1965.

documents. Moreover, in the post-Conciliar era, with the help of the legislation contained in these documents, many Catholic bishops and clergymen caused almost every aspect of Catholic sacred music to be replaced by musical and liturgical practices that are the exact opposite of those enjoined in the motu proprio of 1903.

In order to explain these aberrations, "conservative" Catholics continue to argue that the suppression of traditional Catholic liturgy and sacred music is being caused by various clergymen "abusing" liturgical laws, and not from any obrogation or abrogation contained in the Conciliar and post-Conciliar documents. They believe this because the documents appear, on the surface, to reaffirm the laws of the traditional liturgy. However, a closer examination shows that most of these problems originate *from within* the documents themselves, that is, from loopholes carefully calculated to undermine the apparent traditional-sounding legislation, resulting in a *de facto* obrogation of the traditional laws. Thus, a suppression of the traditional legislation caused by alleged "abuses" is in truth a real, legal change in the way that sacred music (as well as the whole liturgy) is *officially* practiced in the new rite.[26]

---

[26] Yes, there have been some true "abuses," but these generally were "legalized" by Rome after the regulations had been ignored for some length of time – for example, communion in the hand and altar girls. It should also be noted that just because the proper authorities institute changes in the law does not necessarily mean that these laws are good for the Church. At Vatican I, when the Relators of the Deputation of the Faith were discussing the proper understanding of the jurisdictional authority of the pope, they emphasized that popes could only legislate in a manner that would *build up the Body of Christ*, and that they could never licitly use their authority to destroy or harm the Church. Moreover, it should be noted that the Tridentine Mass has never been legally suppressed.

THE CANONICAL STATUS OF THE MOTU PROPRIO SINCE THE NEW CODE OF 1983

In terms of the fourth issue, a change regarding the laws of sacred music comes from Pope John Paul II's new *Code of Canon Law*. This change consists of the exclusion of Canon 1264 of the old 1917 *Code of Canon Law* from the new *Code*. Recall that Canon 1264 of the old code proscribes anything lascivious or impure in sacred music, and provides a firm canonical foundation for the validity of sacred music laws: "All music, whether instrumental or vocal, which contains anything lascivious or impure, must be entirely kept out of Churches. The liturgical laws concerning sacred music shall be observed."[27] With the exclusion of Canon 1264 from the new Code (and no parallel canon to replace it), there is yet another major gap that has eroded the foundation of Church laws designed to uphold the basic principles of Pius X's reform.

CONCLUSION

Thus, in the post-Conciliar era — with the "Spirit of Vatican II" in full swing, national episcopal conferences drunk with power derived illicitly from a false collegiality, clerical and lay rebellion increasingly widespread throughout the Church, and the Conciliar and post-Conciliar documents filled with legal loopholes favoring the neo-Modernist agenda — the great reform of Pope St. Pius X came to a grinding halt. Instead of being used to build up Christ's Church, Church law is now being perverted in order to destroy the traditional laws of sacred music. It is thus imperative that the motu proprio of 1903 be re-established as official law governing Catholic sacred music, and that the opposing "legislation" (which is probably invalid) should be officially overturned.

---

[27] PLSM 515.

Finally, there is a real need to educate "conservative" Catholic daydreamers and wanderers, who, having been led down the primrose path, continue to hold (despite overwhelming evidence to the contrary) that these documents and their legislators are not truly responsible for the liturgical anarchy rampant today in *Novus Ordo* parishes.[28]

---

[28] In the years following the Second Vatican Council, it was not obvious that the documents contained serious flaws. Thus, many early commentators can be forgiven for not understanding the neo-Modernist ploy. Nevertheless, in the last half-century, and in light of numerous studies on the subject, it is apparent that the documents are riddled with more holes than a Swiss cheese. Thus, the current "conservative" Catholic position is factually untenable.

CHAPTER 5
A Brief history of the Implementation of the Reform

THIS CHAPTER WILL BE CONCERNED WITH the historical implementation of the reform from the time of the motu proprio of 1903 to the death of Pius XII. This discussion focuses first on the establishment of diocesan commissions. These commissions are formed to oversee the quality of sacred music in Catholic churches throughout the world, and are best exemplified by the diocesan commission set up in Rome by Pope St. Pius X. The examination also includes Pius's promotion of academic institutions for the training of professional church musicians.

DIOCESAN COMMISSIONS AND THE PROMOTION OF HIGH MUSICAL STANDARDS

One of Pope St. Pius X's greatest wishes was to ensure that the reform be properly implemented in all of the Church's Latin rite dioceses. In order to accomplish this end, Pius X insisted on the establishment of a commission in *every* diocese to monitor the quality of sacred music. Each commission would be responsible, in its respective diocese, for overseeing the choice of compositions, supervising the quality of musicianship, monitoring the performance of sacred music, and executing disciplinary action for those disobeying the principles of the reform. Thus, these diocesan commissions would

become key institutions in the promotion and enforcement of the reform.

Pius's great aspirations were nowhere more evident than in the diocese of the Holy See in Rome itself.
There, Pius desired to see the sacred music of the Church
become an exemplar to the world, so that those visiting
would hear, and be inspired by, the magnificent sounds
of Gregorian chant and sacred polyphony resounding in
her great churches. In order to accomplish this end, Pius
set up a diocesan commission to implement the reform in
Rome. Now by examining the Roman Commission one
can obtain, in a microcosm, the anatomy of the diocesan
institution established for the promotion and mainte-
nance of high sacred music standards. This Roman Commission conforms exactly to the wishes of Pius X in his
quest for sacred music reform.

Pius initiates the reform in Rome on December 8, 1903
with a detailed letter to the vicar general of Rome, Cardinal Respighi. The purpose of this letter is to ensure that
the reform of sacred music in Rome would be accomplished strictly according to the principles contained in
the motu proprio of 1903. The letter is too long to quote
here at length, but some excerpts showing Pius's concern
for *high musical standards* are most revealing. In one passage, Pius complains that there remain many abuses in
Rome itself that need to be corrected:

> Many things must be either corrected or
> removed in the chanting of the Mass, of the Lit-
> any of Loreto, and of the hymns of the Blessed
> Sacrament, but the thing which most demands
> a complete change is the singing of Vespers on
> feast days in the different churches and basilicas.
> The laws of the *Caeremoniale Episcoporum* and
> the beautiful traditions of the classical Roman
> school of music are no longer observed. Instead

of the pious chanting of the clergy, in which the faithful too could take part, endless musical compositions on the words of the Psalms have been substituted, formed in the style of the old theatrical works, most of them of such small value as works of art that they would not be borne even at second-rate secular concerts. The piety and devotion of Christians are certainly not helped by this music, the curiosity of a few less intelligent people may be whetted; but most are only disgusted and scandalised, and wonder that such an abuse should still be tolerated. We desire that these things be entirely suppressed, and that the Vespers be always celebrated according to the liturgical rules that We have laid down.[1]

Later in the same letter, Pius expresses his desire for the correct teaching of sacred music in seminaries and colleges. He also extols the many institutions that have promoted the reform, but is pointed in his criticism of the poor musical standards he has found at other seminaries and colleges:

We desire finally that sacred music be taught with special care in all the Roman seminaries and ecclesiastical colleges, to which so great a number of chosen students come from all parts of the world, to be educated in sacred learning and in a really ecclesiastical spirit. We know, and it is a great consolation to Us, that in many institutions sacred music flourishes so as to make them a model to others. But other seminaries and colleges leave much to be desired in this respect, either through the carelessness of their superiors or through the incapacity and bad taste of the persons who are teachers of singing and directors of sacred music.[2]

---

[1] Pope St. Pius X, Letter to Cardinal Respighi in PLSM 233.
[2] PLSM 233.

On December 29, 1903, under the direction of Pius X, a circular letter authored by Cardinal Pietro Vicario, prefect of the Congregation of Sacred Rites, was sent to the pastors, rectors, superiors of all churches, seminaries, colleges, and ecclesiastical institutions for education in Rome, for the purpose of bringing the motu proprio of 1903, as well as the letter of December 8, 1903, to their attention. This letter also lists the members of the Roman Commission of Sacred Music, and indicates the important role this commission will have in the enforcement of the reform:

> We have enlisted the assistance of the Roman Commission of Sacred Music . . . for the rigorous enforcement of the ordinance; and that availing ourselves of the work the prudent judgment of the same commission [shall undertake], we shall as occasion demands, resort to the practical measures which we deem necessary in each individual case, so that the wise provisions of His Holiness may be fully observed by all concerned.
>
> The Roman Music Commission is composed of the following: Right Rev. Monsignor Lorenzo Perosi, Perpetual Director of the Sistine Chapel. Filippo Capocci, Director and Organist of the Chapel of the Archbasilica of the Lateran. Reverend Doctor Calcedonio Mancini, p.d.m., Consultor of the Sacred Congregation of Rites, for the Liturgical Committee. Baron Rudolph Kanzler, Professor of Gregorian Chant in the School of St. Cecilia, and Secretary of the Pontifical Commission of Sacred Archeology. Alessandro Parisotti, Professor of Harmony and Secretary of the School of Music of the Academy of St. Cecilia. Reverend Father Antonio Rella, Professor of Gregorian Chant. Filippo Mattoni, Singer of the Cappella Giulia of St. Peter's Basilica. (The Reverends Lorenzo Perosi and Antonio Rella are assigned in a special manner to supervise the

> Gregorian Chant in the seminaries and colleges,
> and the ecclesiastical institutions of education.)[3]

This list of illustrious musicians charged by Pius X to supervise musical standards in Rome is truly impressive. The list contains the names of the Catholic Church's top composers, music professors, and sacred music performers active in the Rome of Pius's day. If you have concluded from these quotations that Pius X is very serious about maintaining high musical standards, you are on the right track towards understanding the mind of this great pope.

At this point, however, one should not think that Pius's musical leadership was only manifested in strict commands and acerbic criticisms of bad music and incompetent musicians. Pius also continued to encourage and compliment copiously church musicians and ecclesiastics in many parts of the world for their positive contributions to the reform.[4]

As the reform continued in Rome, a letter from Cardinal Respighi, again under the direction of Pius X, issued further clarifications on the performance aspect of Catholic sacred music in Rome. The document is dated February 2, 1912. Father Hayburn quite succinctly summarizes the content of this letter, which shows the breadth, depth, and bold sweep of the reform, especially in its use of so many important Catholic institutions:

> The document issued by the vicar of Rome, Cardinal Pietro Respighi, gave explicit directions for the performance of ecclesiastical functions and ceremonies. The Italian Association of St. Cecilia helped in the work of restoration.

---

[3] Cardinal P. Vicario in PLSM 234–235.
[4] PLSM 236–238. Pius X wrote many personal letters of praise and gratitude to musicians and ecclesiastics who had accomplished notable results in promoting the reform.

Regulations were established to train students
in seminaries and religious houses. Rules were
given for choir directors, organists, and singers. Norms were laid down for the rectors of
churches and religious houses. Bishops and
superiors were asked to send students to the
Superior School of Sacred Music [later known as
the Pontifical Institute of Sacred Music] where
they could be trained to lead the liturgical and
musical reform for their own dioceses and
orders. An appendix listed the members of the
Roman Commission on Sacred Music and the
functions of that group.[5]

Several quotations from this 1912 document will also
make it abundantly clear that Pius is not about to tolerate
arrogant, self-satisfied amateur incompetents, as well as
their endless and tiresome propagation of musical abuses.
These quotations, which could be multiplied, shall make
clear the *high musical standards* that Pius X willed for
the Church:

> 3. Since not only the rendering of the Grego-
> rian chant but also that of certain ancient and
> modern compositions is left entirely to the
> choir, there is a danger lest, both in the choice
> of pieces and the manner of singing them, the
> ecclesiastical regulations may be infringed; *it is*
> *therefore necessary to make sure that all members*
> *of the choir are technically competent and willing*
> *to observe each and every ecclesiastical regulation,*
> *and work for the application of the Pope's motu*
> *proprio*...[6]
> 4. No choir or schola cantorum can be set
> up in Rome *without previous permission of the*
> *Visità Apostolica, and unless it have at its head*
> *a certified master or conductor and an organist*

---

[5] PLSM 241. In these quotations, all emphases are added.
[6] Cardinal Respighi, Letter of Feb. 2, 1912 in PLSM 242-243.

also approved. The master or conductor of the chapel or schola is mainly responsible to the authorities for any infringement of the ecclesiastical rules on the part of the chapel or schola...[7]

6. No one can exercise in any church or oratory whatever within the city or Diocese of Rome, for any sacred ceremony whatsoever, the function of choirmaster, organist or chorister, *without having obtained a faculty for so doing from the competent ecclesiastical authority, acting on the advice of the Roman Commission for Sacred Music.*

In order to obtain this authorization the following qualities and conditions are necessary: a) *Professional capacity* for sacred music in the function or functions contemplated, *to be confirmed by the usual diplomas, or, in special cases, their equivalents...*

7. The Roman Commission for Sacred Music *will judge of the different qualifications of the candidates for the office of choirmaster, organist or chorister;* and if they think it expedient, *they can demand an examination for each, to prove their artistic capacities.* If the candidates are not as yet sufficiently familiar with Gregorian chant *they cannot take part in any function ... until they obtain the necessary certificate of proficiency.*

8. The Visità Apostolica will have a register of the names of choirmasters, organists, and choristers *recognized as qualified to exercise their art in the Roman churches.*

One could go on with quotation after quotation supporting the thesis that Pius X *mandated* the use of *only* qualified musicians for the service of the liturgy. Now I ask the reader this question: in light of the plethora of evidence adduced, would Pius X allow untrained amateurs

---

[7] This and the following paragraphs are taken from PLSM 243.

to mount the stairs of our Catholic choir lofts and present themselves as choral directors, singers, and organists in God's holy liturgy? Obviously, he was not about to tolerate this sort of abuse.

Yet if we consider the situation today, in all too many traditionalist chapels, mediocre amateurs, along with untrained and musically uneducated persons blissfully reign over wretchedly performed and often poorly chosen "sacred music." (There are notable exceptions, but these are certainly not the norm.) To make matters even worse, these aberrations frequently have the explicit approval of the chapel priest! Meanwhile, *Novus Ordo* bishops, well aware of traditionalist shortcomings with sacred music, now make sure that their "conservative" Catholic churches have trained musicians to ensure that the music is at least reasonably well performed, and thus attractive to their congregations. Unfortunately, this music is usually secular, and therefore not truly Catholic!

Thus, well-informed traditional Catholics must endure a threefold cross: first, "liberal" counter-church apostates performing "pop/rock" music as if it were "sacred music"; second, "conservative" Catholics who, while blindly obeying their bishops, tolerate the use of pianos, guitars, and an abundance of shallow, sentimental "pop" music as "sacred music"; and third, widespread traditionalist ignorance of what traditional Catholic sacred music even is, along with truly substandard and amateurish performances that scandalize the faithful! When will all of these sacrilegious abuses end?

Before leaving this topic, let me emphasize again that the musical standards of the reform were to apply to *all* Catholic Latin rite dioceses, not just the Diocese of Rome. This is because each diocese was to have the equivalent of the Roman Commission of Sacred Music overseeing its practice of Catholic sacred music.

OPPOSITION TO THE REFORM AT THE TIME OF THE MOTU PROPRIO OF 1903

Despite the clarity of the documents and the obvious mandate for high standards issued by Pius X, there were, unfortunately, some voices of opposition to the reform even at the time of its promulgation. As Fr. Hayburn observes:

> The documents issued personally by Pius X and those issued through the Congregation of Sacred Rites were received with great joy by many musicians who had waited a long time for a reform in Church music. Others, who found these changes contrary to their practices and tastes, were reluctant to accept them and began to spread rumors concerning their origin. They claimed that the documents had been obtained with maneuvers and that Pius X had published them, being almost ignorant of what he was doing. Others said that the Pope had been cheated and that he really did not think as they had compelled him to write in the motu proprio. Others laid the blame on the Roman Commission for Sacred Music, saying that this group was imposing itself upon the Pope.[8]

These complaints were relayed to Pius X, who commented on them in an audience given at the Roman Music Commission on July 24, 1914. The meeting was recorded by the *Rassegna Gregoriana*, and a transcript was then obtained by Don Lorenzo Perosi. Perosi related the following about Pius's specific remarks to the audience on the comments of the dissenters:

> He told them not to keep an account of the partisan voices that he knew had been spread to make people believe that in some way he was going to recede from the decisions taken, almost as if

---

[8] PLSM 235–236.

he had been wrong and as if he were not aware of the true situation of the musical problems of Rome and elsewhere. He said exactly: "How can they say that I let myself be influenced by people of these days? I have for twenty years pushed the restoration of sacred music in other places." His Holiness kept on talking of the necessity of the reform, which is a big advantage, both to the liturgy and to the musical art. He said: "I like secular art, I admire Verdi, but not in church."[9]

CATHOLIC UNIVERSITY AND SEMINARY CURRICULA

As we have seen in the documents on the reform in Rome, along with the establishment of the Roman Commission, the evidence shows clearly that Pius X demanded *high musical standards*. Now one of the outstanding features of these documents is the emphasis given to musical academic institutions that would provide the training to produce highly qualified Catholic Church musicians. One of the most important of these institutions will be the Pontifical Institute of Sacred Music.

THE PONTIFICAL INSTITUTE OF SACRED MUSIC

From the very beginning of the reform, Pius and his close friend and musical advisor, the eminent musicologist and church musician Fr. Angelo De Santi, S. J., both contemplated establishing a leading Catholic educational

---

[9] L. Perosi, transcript of the Roman Music Commission meeting of July 24, 1914 in PLSM 236. Pius is here referring to the great Italian composer Giuseppe Verdi (1813–1901). Verdi is remembered for such famous Italian operas as *La Traviata* (1853), *Il Trovatore* (1853), *Aïda* (1871), *Otello* (1887), *Falstaff* (1893), and many others. Pius admired Verdi's music as secular art with integrity of form, but absolutely refused to allow such music, or any adaptation thereof, into the liturgy of the Church, because it was not true sacred music. Even Verdi's famous *Requiem* does not qualify as true Catholic sacred music, because it contains numerous secular and theatrical elements.

institution that would be the exemplar and center of Catholic musical learning. This aspiration was finally realized when Pius X founded a new school in 1910, with Fr. De Santi as its president. The school was first known as the "Superior School of Sacred Music" and was located in Rome.

Pius was greatly impressed by the progress of the school, and, at the request of Fr. De Santi, in 1914 conferred upon it the title of "Pontifical School." This title granted the school the power to confer diplomas in the name of the Holy See. These diplomas were given for master's and doctoral degrees in three specific areas of study: Gregorian chant, composition, and organ. Pius conferred this new title by a rescript of the secretary of state to Cardinal Gaetano Bisleti. The first paragraph of the rescript indicates Pius's favorable attitude towards this noble musical institution:

> I am very pleased to inform Your Eminence that the Holy Father, Pius X, kindly took into consideration the request made through Your Eminence by Father Angelo De Santi, S. J., general President of the Italian Association of St. Cecilia and President of the Superior School of Sacred Music. Such a request consists in the petition that the above-mentioned School can use the title of "Pontifical," and could have the right to grant public and authorized degrees of ability, of license, and of teaching in the Gregorian chant, and of teaching in sacred composition, and in the organ, to the pupils and to the externs who pass the examinations and become worthy of the title.[10]

After Pius X's death in 1914, the new pontiff, Benedict XV, continued to promote and encourage the reform, including the Pontifical School of Sacred Music. In fact,

---

[10] Rescript to Cardinal Bisleti in PLSM 297.

Benedict XV would leave virtually everything Pius X had decreed for the Pontifical School in effect. Benedict would also give the school new and larger quarters in the Gregorian Room of St. Apollinaris and the adjoining living quarters.

With the advent of Pope Pius XI, the reform continued to be promoted and developed. The development included this Pope's continuing support of the Pontifical School of Sacred Music, which was elevated to a higher status (that is, to a Pontifical Institute) by Pius XI in his motu proprio *Ad musicæ sacræ restitutionem* of November 22, 1922. This motu proprio exhibits a consistent application of the principles articulated in Pius X's motu proprio of 1903.

The motu proprio of 1922 begins with an Introduction that is followed by several numbered articles. The first few articles indicate that the patron of the Pontifical School will be a cardinal of the Church, who will hold the School in his jurisdiction and power. A president will be chosen, and he will be assisted by a body of ten doctors of music, which will comprise the Academic College. The ten doctors of the Academic College will direct the curriculum, and supervise all disciplinary matters.

The heart of the motu proprio of 1922 is contained in numbers 5 through 8.

Number 5 stresses the rigorous examinations entailed in obtaining any of the degrees:

> The Cardinal Patron together with the President and body of ten doctors will be entitled to confer the academic degrees of Bachelor and Doctorate or Master of Gregorian chant, composition of sacred melodies, and organ playing. They shall confer such degrees on those candidates who shall have successfully undertaken both an oral and written examination in the subject matter.
>
> It shall be the duty of this Schola to contribute to the progress of the knowledge of Gregorian

chant, to the progress of the art of composing
the sacred melodies – towards this end the great
masters of polyphony who flourished in the sixteenth century are especially to be studied – and
to the progress of the study of the organ.[11]

Number 6 is particularly interesting in that it not only
indicates the importance of the study of Gregorian chant,
but in mentioning the art of composing sacred melodies,
highly recommends studying the masters of sixteenth-
century classical polyphony.

Number 7 stresses the complete and uncompromising
continuity of this motu proprio of 1922 with the laws contained in Pius X's motu proprio of 1903: "Whatever was set
forth in Pius X's motu proprio concerning sacred music
is to be observed as sacred law in all the disciplines of the
Schola" [i.e., the Pontifical Institute of Sacred Music].[12]

Number 8 articulates the primary thrust of the *Schola*,
which is to promote the Gregorian chant; for after all,
Gregorian chant is the highest model of sacred music,
and all endeavors of sacred polyphony must be grounded
in the knowledge of and proficiency in Gregorian chant:

> All the various functions of the Schola shall have
> one basic concern: the support and advance-
> ment of the Gregorian chant. Therefore no one
> will be allowed to achieve any academic degree
> in any study whatsoever, unless he be already
> proficient in Gregorian chant.[13]

In 1931, Pope Pius XI reorganized the curricula of all
the pontifical seminaries and universities. These changes
were promulgated in the apostolic constitution, *Deus Scientiarum Dominus* of May 24, 1931. The relevant parts
of this constitution are in Title III: Concerning Studies.

---

[11] Pope Pius XI, motu proprio of 1922 in PLSM 299.
[12] PLSM 299.
[13] PLSM 299.

Under this title is no. 1: General Method of Teaching. In this section, Pius XI identifies two main methods for teaching: one, the historical-critical method, the other, the theoretical-practical method.[14]

In the same year, 1931, Pius XI added other regulations that follow upon *Deus Scientiarum Dominus*. These pertain specifically to the *Schola*, which is now entitled the Pontifical Institute of Sacred Music. In number VIII: Pontifical Institute of Sacred Music, the following detailed description of the curriculum of the Institute is found:

A. *Gregorian chant*

    1. *Principal studies*: a) General Gregorian Theory; b) Aesthetics, Higher Theory, Gregorian Paleography; c) Institutions of the Sacred Liturgy; d) Practice in Gregorian Chant.

    2. *Auxiliary disciplines*: a) History of Music; b) Various Kinds of Psalmody; c) The Art of Correct Singing; d) The Art of Directing

---

[14] Pope Pius XI, Apostolic Constitution: *Deus Scientiarum Dominus*, no. 1: General Method of Teaching in PLSM 301. The "theoretical-practical" method is musicological terminology for what is known today as "music theory," and its practical application to musical exercises, as well as to actual musical compositions. Music theory is one of several subjects of the branch of musicology known as "systematic musicology." In most colleges and universities, both secular and Catholic, music theory is studied first from an analytical perspective. Then, musical compositions are analyzed in order for the student to see the utilization of the principles of theory in actual music by great composers. Finally, the student composes exercises (and later, actual compositions) using the knowledge of the principles he has learned.

The "historical-critical" method is alluding to the other major branch of musicology known as "historical musicology." It is a type of criticism that analyzes a work of art and evaluates it according to the social and historical contexts in which it was produced, as well as the facts surrounding the author's life. The "historical-critical" method is primarily concerned with determining the meaning that a particular work had for its own time. It is just one of several methods used by musicologists in their study of music history.

Gregorian Chant; e) Harmony and Counterpoint; f) The Complementary Arts of Playing
the Organ and Piano; g) The Art of Blending
the Organ with the Gregorian Chant.

3. *Special disciplines and particular courses are
reviewed in their proper statutes.*

B. *Composition of Sacred Melodies*

1. *Principal disciplines*: a) Harmony, Counterpoint, the Fugue; b) The Art of Composing
to Various Musical Forms.

2. *Auxiliary studies*: a) Musicology; b) Sacred
Polyphony According to the Old and Best
Composers; c) The Art of Choir Directing;
d) Norms for Judging Musical Compositions;
e) Symphonic Art (Instrumentation).

3. *Special disciplines and particular courses are
reviewed in their proper statutes.*

C. *The Organ*

1. *Principal disciplines*: a) The Art of Playing the
Organ; this is the principal subject; b) The
Art of Improvising an Accompaniment on
the Organ for the Gregorian Chant; c) Art of
Composing Music for the Organ According
to Ancient and Recent Styles.

2. *Auxiliary disciplines*: a) History, Structure and
Aesthetics of the Organ. The More Illustri-
ous Composers for the Organ; b) Rules for
Teaching How to Play the Organ.

3. *Special disciplines and particular courses are
reviewed in their proper statutes.*[15]

---

[15] Ordinances following on *Deus Scientiarum Dominus*, Title III:
Concerning Studies, VIII: Pontifical Institute of Sacred Music in
PLSM 302. The Composition requirements also included those dis-
ciplines required for the degree in Gregorian chant: (A), (1-a), (c),

This curriculum of the Pontifical Institute is sufficient to prove, beyond all reasonable doubt, that Pius X, Benedict XV, and Pius XI all intended there to be high musical standards for the reform.

SEMINARY SACRED MUSIC CURRICULUM

For Pius X, the Catholic seminary is another key institution for the promotion of the reform. Since after their seminary training most priests will be in a parish where they will be in charge of the sacred liturgy, including sacred music, it is crucial for the success of the reform that priests have proper training in music so that sacred music will be correctly utilized and performed in the liturgy. In order for priests to have good training, however, there must be a good sacred music curriculum in place and operating at each seminary. This is why Pius X insists on an excellent musical curriculum for all Catholic seminaries.

Now the development of the seminary curriculum from the time of Pius X to Pius XII is too complex to examine in detail here. Nevertheless, if we study this curriculum as it matured under Pius XII, we can see a highly developed pedagogy that manifests a high degree of conformity to the principles of Pius X's reforms. This curriculum, along with the rest of Pius's great reform, represents the culmination of over fifty years of organic development before Vatican II brought it all to an abrupt end.

In order to obtain a glimpse of this curriculum, we can consult a circular letter from the Sacred Congregation of Seminaries and Universities issued on November 22,

---

(d). The Organ requirements also included subjects from both the Gregorian chant and Composition degrees: (A), (1-a), (c), (d); (B), (1-a); (A), (2-a), (b), (c), (g); (B), (2-b), (d). These chant requirements were included in both degree programs to make certain that graduates were grounded thoroughly in Gregorian chant.

1957 by Cardinal Giuseppe Pizzardo.[16] This document contains two parts: first, a directive that forms an introduction; and second, the Circular Letter, which amounts to a very detailed syllabus of the entire four-year sacred music curriculum of a Catholic seminary as envisioned by the Congregation. In the introduction, the Cardinal indicates the primary reason for the Circular:

> In recent National and International Congresses the vote was expressed that this same Sacred Congregation [of Seminaries and Universities] would also formulate a detailed program for such teaching. The same request came from Bishops and Seminary Rectors, pointing out the opportunity of handing down precise program outlines, so that said teaching might have an organic, complete and uniform approach.
>
> To this end we are enclosing herewith a program of teaching, compiled with the collaboration of illustrious teachers, experts in this matter both technically and didactically.[17]

The Circular Letter, which contains the seminary syllabus, is entitled: "Program for the Teaching of Sacred Music in the Seminaries of Italy,"[18] and is divided into

---

[16] Incidentally, this date is the 54th anniversary of the promulgation of the motu proprio of 1903.

[17] Circular Letter (with directive) of Cardinal Pizzardo of the Sacred Congregation of Seminaries and Universities in PLSM 310–14. Please note that the Cardinal states that this syllabus is compiled by "illustrious" teachers who are *experts* in terms of technique and teaching skills – not amateurs. Moreover, why is it that some people with a little musical experience and knowledge think that they are "experts" on the subject of music, and thus qualified to give their (usually foolish) musical opinions to genuine experts in sacred music? This never ceases to amaze me.

[18] While the Pontifical Institute for Sacred Music was strictly for advanced study by those with outstanding talent and considerable musical backgrounds, the seminary curriculum envisioned by the Sacred Congregation of Seminaries and Universities began with the

four general parts: first, the elementary level, which is designated *Scuola Media* (Low-High School) and consists of five grades, each of which covers the elementary principles of music theory, practical music, liturgy, and music history. Second, there is the *Corso Liceale* (College; Liceum), which constitutes the college level. This consists of four grades that each includes the study of Gregorian chant, "figured music" (i.e., polyphony), liturgy, and the history of music. The third part is designated "Theological Course," and comprises four grades each of which covers issues in Gregorian chant, as well as the history of music from a Catholic theological perspective. The fourth part, "Study of the Instrument," is a recommendation that seminarians study the piano as a preparation for organ studies later in the curriculum. This last curriculum follows the conventional methods of piano and organ pedagogy.[19]

The "Program for the Teaching of Sacred Music to the Seminaries of Italy" (the syllabus for the training of seminary students in sacred music), as well as the curriculum of the Pontifical Institute of Sacred Music, should put to rest all arguments that Pius X, and the other twentieth century pre-Conciliar popes, were not concerned with *high musical standards* for musicians serving the Church's liturgy.

---

fundamentals of music, and then systematically progressed from the high school level to the senior college level during the four years of seminary studies. Even a quick perusal of this curriculum shows that, at the level of the *Corso Liceale* and beyond, it was similar to most undergraduate music curricula of the time, as well as those now current in colleges and universities, only with, of course, a far better coverage of Catholic theology, liturgy, and sacred music than that found in contemporary secular colleges and universities.
[19] This is so future priests will be able to accompany the Gregorian chant for the liturgy in the parish church. The term "figured music" is referring here to polyphonic music. Indirectly, it also implies the subjects concerned with the study of polyphony, such as harmony, counterpoint, form, and the fundamentals of music.

With the dawn of Vatican II there was hope that the reform would continue to develop and flourish as it had under pre-Conciliar popes. Unfortunately, in the 1960s, the reform would enter a nightmare from which it has still not emerged.

THE DEMISE OF THE TRADITIONAL LITURGY AND CATHOLIC SACRED MUSIC

Although the roots of the revolution extend far back to the early part of the twentieth century, the sad story of the demise of Pius X's great reform is first clearly manifested with the convocation of the Second Vatican Council (1962–1965) by "good" Pope John XXIII.[20] The story ends with the almost complete destruction of not only the traditional Catholic liturgy, but the whole body of traditional Catholic sacred music as well.

SACROSANCTUM CONCILIUM: "CAPSTONE" OR GUILLOTINE?

One of several infamous documents to come from Vatican II is *Sacrosanctum Concilium* of 1965, which contains the principal legislation on the sacred liturgy. To

---

[20] The whole history of the reform of sacred music should also be understood in the context of the Liturgical Movement begun by Dom Guéranger in France, the father of the reform of Gregorian chant at the Solesmes monastery. This authentic Catholic movement was, of course, vigorously promoted by Pius X, not only in the motu proprio of 1903, but also with other pieces of superb legislation on the liturgy. The Liturgical Movement was gradually subverted, both before and after Vatican II, by many radicals, such as Dom Lambert Beauduin, Dom Odo Casel, Giacomo Cardinal Lercaro, Fr. Yves Congar, and, of course, the big spider at the center of the Vatican II web of liturgical reforms, the ubiquitous Fr. (and later Archbishop) Annibale Bugnini. For more on the subversion of the Liturgical Movement, both before and after Vatican II, see the excellent book by Rev. Fr. Didier Bonneterre entitled: *The Liturgical Movement: From Dom Guéranger to Annibale Bugnini, or The Trojan Horse in the City of God* (Kansas City, MO: The Angelus Press, 2002).

the minds of "conservative" Catholic church musicians, *Sacrosanctum Concilium* is looked upon as a "capstone," a crowning glory of Catholic sacred music legislation that brings to a culmination the great reform initiated by Pope St. Pius X in his motu proprio of 1903. But well-informed readers know that the evidence brought forth in such works as Michael Davies's three-volume *Liturgical Revolution*, Dr. Thomas Droleskey's *G. I. R. M Warfare*, and Romano Amerio's *Iota Unum*, not to mention numerous other publications, make it clear that *Sacrosanctum Concilium* together with other post-Conciliar liturgical documents was designed to decapitate the traditional liturgy, not to be its crowning glory or "capstone."[21]

The destruction of the liturgy and sacred music came from within the ranks of the Church by revolutionaries using their positions of power to force a religious "revolution" on the faithful. This revolution has plunged the Church into a crisis unprecedented in its entire history. The revolution was accomplished with the help of documents, both Conciliar and post-Conciliar, which, in terms of sacred music, thoroughly undermined virtually every precept that Pius X articulated in his motu proprio of 1903. Today, in *Novus Ordo* churches, the liturgy and the treasury of Catholic sacred music are in a shambles. We can only pray that some future council, led by true Catholic prelates and a pope of the caliber of St. Pius X, will undo the appalling damage that neo-Modernists have accomplished in this most unfortunate post-Conciliar era.

---

[21] For further supporting argumentation, see Peter Kwasniewski, "*Sacrosanctum Concilium*: The Ultimate Trojan Horse," *Crisis Magazine*, June 21, 2021; on the problems in that document's chapter on sacred music, see Garrett Meyer, "'Other Things Being . . . Equal'? A Critique of *Sacrosanctum Concilium* 116," *New Liturgical Movement*, October 14, 2024.

It is important to understand that not every possible aspect of Pius X's great reform has been covered here. The focus of the discussion has been on the principles of the motu proprio of 1903 itself, because an understanding of these principles is crucial to any attempt to restore traditional Catholic sacred music, now, or in the future. Nor is this essay by any means the last word on Pius's reform. There have been many sources written on the reform from various perspectives, as well as those that deal with specific and/or controversial issues. All of these sources should be read and considered.

This brings to a conclusion our examination of the principles of the motu proprio, its canonical aspects, and a brief survey of the implementation of the reform. We turn now to a discussion of what traditional Catholics, inspired by Pope Saint Pius X's true reform, can do to restore the sacred music of the Church given the present situation.

Chapter 6
A Plan to Restore True Catholic Sacred Music

ANY ATTEMPT TO RESTORE CATHOLIC sacred music in our time is bound to be a difficult undertaking fraught with numerous obstacles principally caused by misguided prelates within the Church, and assisted by their minions among the clergy and lay people. Nevertheless, the best plan for restoring sacred music in the Church is to revive, as much as possible, the reform that Pope St. Pius X initiated in 1903, since this reform is like a great blueprint that contains all of the important elements of a true and thorough restoration of Catholic liturgical music.

Pius X had a distinct advantage in his time given the relatively healthy state of the Church and society in 1903. Gone today, however, is the rich musical cultural milieu of Pius's day, the widespread use of the Tridentine liturgy, the diocesan commissions, pontifical music schools, and a reform assisted by numerous institutions in the ecclesiastical-hierarchical order. This is why any restoration of the traditional liturgy and sacred music in our time will be a truly difficult (but not impossible) task. Moreover, unless a new council is called, and a true reform initiated from within the Catholic Church by that council, this restoration will likely be very slow.

Nevertheless, there are some things that can be done today to at least preserve, cultivate, and perpetuate the treasures of Catholic sacred music through this very dark time. The most important thing to remember here is that we must work to revive as much of the reform of Pope St. Pius X as possible in order to advance this restoration of sacred music. The following suggestions for initiating the revival of the reform are based on the principles of the reform, and come from my own many years of experience in the field of Catholic sacred music.

A UNIFIED PLAN FOR THE REVIVAL OF THE REFORM

In order to begin a revival of Pius X's reform, it is imperative that traditionalists have a unified approach to that revival. This unified approach is found in the "blueprint" that is Pius X's reform. Obviously, we must continue to invoke the help of Our Lord Jesus Christ and His Mother, Mary, by prayers, acts of reparation, and supplication for help in this great task. The next step is to have an intimate knowledge of Pius X's reform. The more one knows and understands the traditional teaching and practice of Catholic sacred music, the better he will be able to implement a revival of the reform.

This can be done in spite of the many misinformed and recalcitrant prelates who oppose the traditional practices (and doctrines) of the Church. The requisite knowledge (i.e., the "blueprint") can be obtained by reading not only Pius X's writings on sacred music, but also reading the many learned documents written on sacred music by pre-Conciliar popes, cardinals, the Congregation of Sacred Rites, and others. Fortunately, most of these documents exist today in good translations. Many books have also been written on the reform, such as Fr. Hayburn's *Papal Legislation on Sacred Music*, which contains an extraordinary wealth of information on most aspects of Pius X's reform. The present book is also an attempt to provide an overview and starting point for those who are interested in contributing to a revival of the reform. Moreover, the knowledge required for the revival of Pius's reform includes a great deal of practical musical knowledge obtained by diligent practice and study.[1] This last point leads to the next step in the revival: musical education.

MUSICAL EDUCATION

Fortunately, the reform of Pius X left us with documents that contain an intimate knowledge of the various musical curricula for the education of Catholic musicians. In chapter 5 of this book, these various curricula have been discussed in detail; these curricula provide an excellent model on which to base a revival of the reform in terms of sacred music education.

Music is a complex art requiring many years of dedicated practice and study under the careful supervision of truly qualified and professional music teachers. After obtaining a working knowledge of Pius's reform, one should (if he has not already done so) give priority to obtaining vocal instruction. We should always remember that the Church teaches that "singing must always be the chief thing,"[2] especially since the Gregorian chant, one of the greatest of all vocal arts, is to have pride of place in the sacred liturgy. Thus, vocal cultivation should be given first priority, regardless of whether one's goal is to be a chorister or a choirmaster.[3] However, where does

---

[1] There are simply no substitutes for hard work and diligent practice if one is to acquire a real proficiency in music.

[2] MP in PLSM 229.

[3] Even if you already have some experience singing in choirs, or have even had some vocal instruction, whether you aspire to be a choirmaster or a chorister, you should continue to cultivate the voice through private, one-on-one vocal instruction.

one find good vocal training? More importantly, in what does good vocal training consist? Let us begin with the first question.

One can obtain private vocal training from colleges, universities, independent music schools, and by teachers giving lessons from their homes.[4] If one is contemplating going to college, my recommendation would be to major in music with voice as your principal instrument. Contemporary colleges and universities generally will provide good musical training in one's principal or major instrument, as well as competent training in music history, music theory, ear training, sight singing, participation in ensembles, keyboard training, and the like. Information on prices and instructors can be obtained on the Internet, by contacting college and university music departments. Even if music will not be one's primary vocation, it is relatively easy to "double major" in music and another subject. One could even major in his career field and "minor" in music, although the musical requirements are not as extensive as those required for music majors.

THE ART OF *BEL CANTO* SINGING

Regarding the second question, good vocal training can be summed up in two words: *bel canto*. These two Italian words mean literally: "beautiful singing."[5] It is

---

[4] Make sure that you check the credentials of teachers giving any kind of musical instruction, particularly those giving instruction out of their home. Teachers who give lessons from their home may be perfectly well qualified, but sometimes they are not. Ask for a resume, or something that provides you with information on their backgrounds, such as where they have taught, what degrees they hold, where they went to school, with whom they studied, whether they belong to any well-known musical organizations in your city, and the like.

[5] The term "bel canto" designates a school of vocal technique initially developed by the Church, and later by Italian opera composers. It is used throughout the seventeenth, eighteenth, and

the classic art of correct vocal singing in which a pow-
erful, resonant, flexible, wide ranging, and beautiful
tone using a minimum of air is produced.[6] This way of
singing grew out of centuries of vocal cultivation in the
Church (and later in the opera house), and reached its
florescence in the eighteenth century. It continued to be

---

nineteenth centuries in not only Italian opera, but also by opera
composers of other countries. It continues, of course, to be used
in modern performances of operas. But it should be stressed that
bel canto technique need not be restricted to opera compositions
only. One can use the benefits of bel canto vocal technique even
in singing Gregorian chant, and without sounding like an opera
singer. I will have more to say about adapting bel canto technique
to Catholic sacred music near the end of this book.

[6] When I say a minimum amount of air, I am referring to the fact
that a properly trained bel canto practitioner can sing his loudest
tone right in front of a lit candle and not make the flame flicker.
I studied with three voice teachers, and my teacher from Holland
was by far the best voice instructor I ever had. I studied with him
for four years. When he told me that a good bel canto singer should
be able to sing his or her loudest note (on an open vowel) and not
make the flame of the candle flicker, I was polite, but deep down
extremely skeptical. Now you must realize that this man had a
voice that could range from incredibly stentorian to extremely
quiet. When he demonstrated his "candle trick" in front of me,
with his voice at full volume blaring out in front of a candle flame
that behaved as if it were in absolutely calm air, I quickly became
a believer. A while later I, myself, was able to do the same thing
with the candle, after, of course, much diligent practice. Now if
I can do this, just about anyone with some talent and the desire
to apply themselves can do it just as well. In addition, a good bel
canto vocalist can easily sustain a pitch without a breath for at
least 20 seconds.

Some famous bel canto singers could even hold a tone for 45
seconds or more, without taking even the slightest breath. This is
because the amount of air used to create any pitch at any volume is
very miniscule in the world of the bel canto singer. Outside of this
world, singer's voices are usually "breathy," they cannot complete
relatively short phrases without gasping for air, and they often
sing without a true vibrato.

Some examples of famous bel canto practitioners include
Luciano Pavarotti, Placido Domingo, Enrico Caruso, Elizabeth
Schwarzkopf, and Maria Callas, among others.

utilized in the nineteenth and twentieth centuries, but it has suffered a decline over the past two centuries.[7]

Although bel canto is most often associated with the cultivation of the "operatic voice," this is not entirely accurate. A well-trained voice is a well-trained voice, regardless of whether one primarily sings opera or sacred music. That is, while the bel canto voice can be modified to sing sacred music without "sounding operatic," that same voice is also easily modified to sing operatic music as well. It all depends upon the style of the music to be performed.[8] In addition, many people think that voice training will "change their voice," as if to imply some negative vocal attribute will be acquired in the course of vocal training. This is not true. If anything, bel canto training will not only prolong the health of the voice, avoiding such frequent problems as phonasthenia,[9] it

---

[7] Many scholars and voice teachers lament the decline in the use of bel canto principles and technique in today's world.

[8] The way that one modifies the voice is to use a slower vibrato for choral singing in church (which also allows the voice to "blend" with the other singers in the choir), and, if in a theater, to use a faster vibrato to sing operatic style music. Since the bel canto voice is the quintessence of flexibility, it is a very easy matter to slow down or speed up the vibrato. Moreover, one can use what is known as *mezza voce* (restrained voice) along with a slower vibrato. When singing Gregorian chant this way, few would ever imagine that you could also sing a piece from an opera, if you so desired. Thus, using one's bel canto training to adapt to the exigencies of sacred music allows the church musician to have virtually all of the benefits of bel canto technique, but without sounding like an opera singer.

[9] *Phonasthenia* is a vocal term indicating various weaknesses of the voice, such as the inability to blend the various registers of the voice, the inability to sustain a vibrato, and the like. Incidentally, those who advocate that the voice should be trained "without using a vibrato" should be avoided like the plague. I would also politely dismiss myself from the care of any voice teacher who told me that "early music" (such as Gregorian chant, 16th century polyphony, etc.) should be sung with "no vibrato." Simply put, these people do not have it right, and are unwittingly setting the student up for problems with various types of phonasthenia in the near future.

will enhance the quality of the singing voice and the speaking voice as well, ensuring a healthy voice well into old age.[10]

Several caveats, however, are in order for bel canto training. First, there is much misinformation today regarding the exact principles of how to train the voice according to bel canto principles. For that matter, there is much misinformation and confusion about voice training in general. This can be very discouraging for beginners searching for a good voice teacher. Nevertheless, the prospective vocalist should not lose heart, for here is where correct knowledge can overcome seemingly insurmountable problems. Furthermore, this is why even a rudimentary understanding of bel canto is so important, and can be a very good guide for the beginner.[11]

In terms of vocal knowledge, the works of Cornelius L. Reid are to be highly recommended. Reid has written three books on the art of bel canto: *Bel Canto: Principles and Practices*; *The Free Voice: A Guide to Natural Singing*; and *Voice: Psyche and Soma*. The first work is a comprehensive history of the development of bel canto singing. The second work is a detailed exposition of the art of training the voice according to bel canto principles. The third work is a study of the psychological complexities of vocal training.[12] It should also be emphasized that

---

[10] My Dutch voice teacher always emphasized the importance of how the speaking voice and the singing voice complemented one another. In reality, the speaking voice helps the singing voice to be a better singing voice, and the singing voice helps the speaking voice be a better speaking voice. I know that this sounds strange, but it is true.

[11] The beginner should not be discouraged, for by doing a little study, using common sense, and praying a lot, he or she will be able to find their way to a good voice teacher. Moreover, do not worry if the teacher is not perfect. No teacher is perfect; just practice, attend lessons faithfully, study, use common sense, and pray.

[12] Just a warning: do not attempt to teach yourself on your own

one should *never* attempt to learn bel canto without a competent voice teacher. To do otherwise, or try to be "self-taught," is to invite vocal disaster. One should also never take "group" vocal instruction. Private, one-on-one instruction with a competent voice instructor is the only way to learn the art of bel canto.

THE ART OF SINGING GREGORIAN CHANT AND CLASSICAL POLYPHONY

Once the student has begun vocal training with a competent instructor, he should also begin to learn the art of singing Gregorian chant. Singing the chant along with vocal training is an excellent way to develop one's skill as a vocalist and church musician. Again, the guidance of a knowledgeable, professionally trained, traditionalist choirmaster with extensive experience in singing Gregorian chant is most valuable to the student of Catholic sacred music.

After gaining experience with singing Gregorian chant, the student should then begin to learn the classical polyphony of the great sixteenth-century composers,

---

with a book, no matter how good the book is. Here is where many people go off the track. Please realize that we hear ourselves different from the way other people hear us. (We usually sound good to ourselves, until we hear our voices on a tape recorder and then realize the awful truth.) This is because we hear ourselves through bone conduction, that is, we hear our voices through the bones in our skull, and by the reverberations bouncing off the walls when inside a building. When other people hear us, they do not hear us through bone conduction. Thus, they hear us differently from the way we hear ourselves. Because of this tendency to believe our voices sound good, many people conclude that they do not need vocal training. This is a huge mistake. Do not fall for this. Only a well-trained voice teacher can guide you on the path to correct vocal technique, because not only can they hear your voice as others hear you, but they also know the correct sounds to listen for, which then guide them in their training of your voice. This is why a good book cannot, of itself, teach a student correct vocal technique.

such as Palestrina, Victoria, Byrd, and other celebrated masters of sacred polyphony. This should be done in a choir led by an experienced traditionalist choirmaster. Then, under the guidance of the choirmaster, the student should experience some modern works that conform to the Church's principles of good sacred music. This last includes the many traditional four-part hymn settings.

Regarding organists, they too should take vocal instruction along with organ studies, because again, Catholic sacred music is primarily a vocal art. In addition, even when the organ is used, it often accompanies chant and other vocal music when not used to play standard solo sacred organ works. It is also important to note that organ lessons should be preceded by at least four years of piano instruction. Both piano and organ instruction should be taken from qualified experts in their respective fields. One should not take either organ or piano instruction from any teacher without at least a B. A. degree in music (or some equivalent), and with piano or organ as their principal instrument. Preferably, one should take instruction from a teacher with a B. A. degree in piano or organ performance.

THE ART OF CHORAL CONDUCTING AND CHOIR ETIQUETTE

The musical background of those aspiring to be choirmasters should include competent instruction in piano, organ, voice, conducting, music history, music theory, a broad knowledge of Western choral music, a sound understanding of the Catholic liturgy, a basic knowledge of the Latin language, and a good deal of experience leading choirs in the traditional liturgy. Here is where traditional parish or chapel priests should be especially careful to hire only choirmasters with this kind of background. Again, if a prospective Catholic choirmaster has a B. A.

in choral conducting (or preferably a graduate degree in choral conducting), and adequate experience in directing choirs in traditional Catholic liturgies, he should be hired.[13] It is a mistake to hire musicians without professional training, and who have little understanding of Catholic sacred music. In this situation, it is strictly the blind leading the blind, with ultimately disastrous results. Once the priest has chosen a qualified choirmaster, he can then be reasonably certain that the choirmaster will hire qualified organists, audition and accept only the best choristers, choose the best works from the repertory, and provide the Mass liturgy with great sacred music that is correctly performed. In this situation, the music will give honor and glory to God, and dispose the congregation to the great wealth of graces from the traditional Mass.[14]

Once the choir is established, rehearsals should be held at least once a week for at least two hours, with a brief "warm-up" rehearsal preceding the Mass on Sundays.[15] On the chosen weekday, the rehearsal should always begin and end with prayer, for example to such saints as St. Gregory the Great, St. Pius X, St. Cecilia, and St. Thomas Aquinas, and the Hail Mary, Our Father, and lesser doxology.

Choir etiquette should be rigorously enforced. This

---

[13] It is important to hire *only* practicing traditional Catholics for the post of choirmaster. Organists and choristers should also be practicing traditional Catholics as well. The only exception I can see with choristers and organists is allowing the participation of someone formally preparing to be brought into the Church as a convert.

[14] It is possible for a church musician to be qualified without possessing an earned degree from an accredited institution. But the chapel or parish priest should be sufficiently trained himself in music in order to determine whether a candidate is sufficiently qualified; if the priest is not qualified himself, he should bring in someone with proper credentials to interview and audition a candidate before hiring him as a choirmaster.

[15] This two-hour rehearsal should include at least one break.

means that if the rehearsal is taking place in the choir loft, or any part of the main church, all the reverence and respect that is shown by the faithful when in church should be followed by the members of the choir, including the director. The rehearsal is not a time for socializing, joking, showing off, or other such things. It is a time for serious study and practice, and, most importantly, for prayer. This is because when one sings sacred music with texts, he is praying twice. Moreover, church musicians should never forget that the rehearsal, as well as the performance on Sunday, is taking place in the house of God—not in a concert hall, and not in a theater. Singers should also have due respect for their director and follow his or her requests. Singers who mock or make fun of the conductor, or who carry on conversations with their fellow singers during rehearsal, should be warned, and if they do not heed that warning, be dismissed from the choir. This is not the place for proud and arrogant singers.

Why is choir etiquette such a serious issue? The reason is that the Devil *despises* true Catholic sacred music to a very great degree, and uses every available means to cause strife and division in the choir. Singers and choir directors should be acutely aware of this truth, and use every technique to counter the inevitable onslaught of Lucifer and his minions. The best way to counter the attack from Hell is to: a) pray for guidance and protection; b) follow God's laws and Catholic precepts faithfully; c) adhere to the sacred music principles of Pius X to the letter; d) work hard to acquire the requisite musical knowledge and training; and e) cultivate a sincere and true Catholic humility.[16]

---

[16] I am always amused by choir singers who attempt to act humble on the outside, but whose real state of mind is anything but humble. They think they fool the choirmaster, but the joke is on them.

PRIESTLY SUPPORT

It is certainly imperative and essential that every traditionalist priest support the revival of the reform wholeheartedly. This also means that every priest should become knowledgeable regarding the nature of Pius X's reform. If a priest is not a professionally trained musician, he should especially consult the expertise of a reputable choirmaster who is both a traditional Catholic and a professionally trained musician with genuine expertise (as evidenced by proper credentials) in Catholic sacred music. To rely on amateurish, outdated, incomplete, and/ or wrong musical information when choosing church musicians is to invite bad sacred music into the Church.[17] Moreover, the choice of a choirmaster is the most important decision a priest will make if he desires to revamp properly the music in his church or chapel. Once he has made his choice, it is imperative that he support the decisions of his choirmaster, as long as those decisions are in conformity with the principles of the reform.[18]

---

[17] A priest once told me that sacred music was too expensive, and thus not worth supporting, because once it was heard, it was gone, and that money paid to the musicians who performed it was thus not very well spent. This, of course, is an example of a very curious attitude. It is born of an unreasonable pragmatism that completely misses the wonderfully beneficial spiritual effects of sacred music, as well as the need to have the faithful exposed to true sacred music during the Catholic liturgy. If you are wondering why there is so much bad music in the world and in the Church today, you need only look to clerics and others like this one who hold such shortsighted views.

[18] I have seen how choirmasters have tried to change the abject state of sacred music in certain churches, but with very poor results. This is because those singers who had no training, and who insisted on remaining without seeking vocal instruction, would complain bitterly to the priest that the choirmaster was "persecuting" them because he would not let them sing without seeking improvement in their voices. Unfortunately, many priests would side with the singers, unwittingly causing the problem either to remain unresolved or to become much worse.

CONTROVERSIAL AND DISPUTED ISSUES
REGARDING THE REFORM

As alluded to previously, there are problems with later pre-Conciliar legislation from the reign of Pope Pius XII, in which there seem to be certain deviations from the legislation contained in Pius X's motu proprio of 1903. Although we cannot delve into all of these controversies in this work, nevertheless, the reader should be aware of at least some of them, and take the time to understand both sides of the problem. Two examples of significant controversies have been selected for discussion. The phrase "significant controversies" means that many scholars believe that these issues involve a genuine break with the traditional sacred music practice of the Church.

Let us begin with liturgical settings that utilize orchestral accompaniment. These sorts of settings do not occur for the most part until the early seventeenth century and beyond. They include the works of famous composers from the Baroque era, such as Claudio Monteverdi and Alessandro Scarlatti; from the Classical period with Masses by Joseph Haydn, Wolfgang Amadeus Mozart, and Ludwig van Beethoven; and from the Romantic era, with settings by such composers as Charles Gounod, Giuseppe Verdi, Anton Bruckner, and many others.

Now the *Instruction* of 1958 allows a more liberal use of orchestral Masses than Pius X permits. However, as seen in

---

A good choir director should have a policy of auditioning prospective singers. This is particularly important if the previous choir consisted largely of bad singers with bad attitudes. It is no violation of the Catholic virtue of charity to insist on reasonable auditions as a way to build a good choir. This is especially true if the choirmaster encourages singers to obtain vocal instruction, and audition again if they did not pass the first time. However, if the priest will not back up the choirmaster in his just endeavor, then it is all over. Only disaster after disaster will follow, with the choir becoming a hotbed of strife, contention, and, worst of all, bad sacred music.

the motu proprio of 1903, Pius insists that sacred music is primarily vocal, and that instruments other than the organ are considered exceptional. These latter are only to be utilized for solemn celebrations, such as high feasts, and then only with special permission from the local Ordinary.[19]

However, Pius's prohibitions were not due to a lack of appreciation for these compositions. For in terms of vocal/instrumental sacred works, it is well known that Pius X himself admired the sacred works of the Venetian School.[20] This is not surprising given that Pius X, when he was cardinal-patriarch of Venice, was well acquainted with the great works of the Venetian masters, whose compositions were composed for, and performed in, the great Church of St. Mark's in Venice. These works are truly great Catholic sacred compositions that conform quite well to the principles of good sacred music.[21] The Venetian masterpieces are highly recommended for very high feasts; the only practical drawback is that they require a large ensemble of instruments, as well as multiple choirs in large performing spaces.

---

[19] This restriction may be considered wise given the abuse of secular instrumental music at the time; nevertheless, historical research indicates that a lot of Renaissance vocal music was discreetly accompanied by instruments such as the organ, the lute or archlute or theorbo, the viola da gamba, and on more splendid occasions, sackbuts and cornets. These early instruments blend in well with voices and do not create the distracting effect of the later orchestral Masses. One might argue that they are as permissible as voices.

[20] The "Venetian School" refers to a style of composition cultivated by composers associated with the church (now cathedral) of St. Mark's in Venice, Italy. The style is noted for its antiphonal effects, many brass instruments, and the use of "split" choruses (*cori spezzati*). The composers of the Venetian School included such illustrious names as Adrian Willaert (c. 1490-1562), Cipriano de Rore (1516-1565), Claudio Merulo (1533-1604), Andrea Gabrieli (c. 1510-1586), his nephew Giovanni Gabrieli (c. 1553-1612), and many others.

[21] This love for the music of the Venetian School is further evidence of Pope St. Pius X's impeccable taste in, and knowledge of, Catholic sacred music.

Another controversial issue involves the assertion, found in the *Instruction* of 1958, that Gregorian chant should be favored above all types of polyphonic sacred music. Now there are no statements in the other documents on the reform that an all-Gregorian chant liturgy is to be the preferred norm. Yet, in paragraph 16 of the *Instruction* of 1958, this very thesis is clearly articulated:

> Gregorian chant is the sacred chant, proper and principal of the Roman Church. Therefore, not only can it be used in all liturgical actions, but unless there are mitigating circumstances, it is preferable to use it *instead of other kinds of sacred music.*[22]

Not only is this thesis nowhere to be found in the motu proprio of 1903, it is clearly contrary to historical precedent, where, at the Council of Trent, there was an attempt by two misguided Council Fathers to get the Council of Trent to outlaw all forms of sacred music except Gregorian chant. According to the historical documents, however, these two prelates never mounted much of an offensive against polyphony, and their proposal was easily defeated by the vast majority of Council Fathers, including one famous Father who led the fight against eliminating polyphonic music from the liturgy, Cardinal Carlo Borromeo, now known today as St. Charles Borromeo. Yet, sadly, we find this gratuitous, time-dishonored, and unreasonable proposition in what many consider the crowning document of the reform: the *Instruction* of 1958.

There are many arguments against the notion of a preference for an all-Gregorian chant liturgy. For now, let it be said that the historical practice of the Church overwhelmingly contradicts this specious assertion, and therefore, we ought to slam the door on this loophole and

---

[22] *Instruction* of 1958 in PLSM 360; emphasis added.

secure it with a lock that even Houdini could not break.

I do not want to give the reader the impression that I am condemning this document in its entirety. I am not. This instruction comes toward the end of the reign of Pius XII, the last of the pre-Conciliar Popes to rule the Church before Pope John XXIII. It comes many years after Pius X initiated his reform, and therefore includes many wise provisions and, in some cases, enunciates a more explicit understanding of Pius's reform. Thus, it should be read, understood, and, where there are no deviations from Pius's reform, utilized. However, it should also be understood that there is probable cause for investigating the charge that Archbishop Annibale Bugnini, the great architect of the *Novus Ordo Missae*, had influenced some of the legislation contained in this document. Is there any basis for this suspicion? It seems to me that there is, for Bugnini was very active as professor and secretary in numerous liturgically important positions in the Vatican of the 1950s.[23] For example, he was appointed Secretary to Pius XII's Commission for Liturgical Reform in 1948. He was made a Professor of Liturgy in the Pontifical *Propaganda Fide* University in 1949. In 1955, he was appointed professor of Liturgy at the Pontifical Institute of Sacred Music; he was made a Consultor to the Sacred Congregation of Rites in 1956; and in 1957, he was appointed Professor of Sacred Liturgy in the Lateran University.[24]

---

[23] According to Michael Davies in the second volume of his Liturgical Revolution: *Pope Paul's New Mass*. According to Peter Kwasniewski, by 1958 Pius XII was gravely ill and others were "running the show" at the Vatican: see his articles "Lights and Shadows in the Pontificate of Pius XII," *OnePeterFive*, September 22, 2021, and "Coincidences During the Reign of Pius XII? Political Background to Vatican II and Liturgical Changes," *LifeSiteNews*, May 25, 2021.
[24] See Davies, *Pope Paul's New Mass*, 527-28; for a recent and fuller account of his life and career, see Yves Chiron, *Annibale Bugnini: Reformer of the Liturgy*, trans. John Pepino (Brooklyn, NY: Angelico Press, 2018).

Now it does not take a Sherlock Holmes to figure out that Bugnini could easily have influenced the contents of a document such as the *Instruction* of 1958. He certainly was influential enough in high liturgical circles in the Vatican of 1958. While this is circumstantial evidence and does not prove he was responsible for the specific aberrations that I have pointed out, it certainly raises many red flags, and thus gives us good reason to continue to investigate this suspicion.

SACRED MUSIC REPERTORIES

In terms of sacred music repertories, the most practical Gregorian chant book for choirmasters today is the *Liber Usualis*, which contains most of the commonly used chants from both the Mass and the Divine Office. I also recommend the collection of psalm tones of the Propers entitled: *Proper of the Mass for the Entire Ecclesiastical Year*, by Rev. Carlo Rossini. These are indispensable for High Masses, since they contain short psalm-tone versions of proper chants that can replace a chant from the *Liber Usualis* that may be too difficult for the choir to sing in its full version.

For classical polyphony, the motets and Masses of Palestrina, Victoria, and Byrd are ideal for performing this style of music in the liturgy. Lists of composer works, biographies, and a wealth of other information are contained in *The New Grove Dictionary of Music and Musicians*, in twenty volumes. This dictionary can be found in large public libraries as well as the music libraries of colleges and universities. Music libraries of local colleges and universities will also contain editions of the complete works of major composers of Western classical music. The *New Grove* dictionary is also an indispensable guide for modern sacred music compositions as well.

SOME FINAL THOUGHTS

The task before us is daunting as we embark on the revival of a reform that has been all but destroyed over the last sixty years. In this quest, it is imperative that church musicians follow all of the principles of Pius's reform, and at the same time reject all principles that conflict with Pius's words.[25] There is a need to restore correctly performed Catholic sacred music not only for the true purposes of sacred music, but also as a leaven in a society that has become evil, secular, and spiritually

---

[25] The advice of all the pre-Conciliar Popes, from Pius X to Pius XII, is that if a piece of sacred music cannot be performed reasonably well, then it should *not be performed*. Many readers will probably want to argue that because we are in exceptional circumstances, standards can be sacrificed based on the "reasoning" that goes: "better to have some music even if it sounds amateurish, than to have no music at all." But one should remember that a Tridentine Mass, such as a Low Mass, can be done without any music and still be valid, licit, and spiritually beneficial. True, a High Mass, being essentially a sung Mass, must have music to be licit. However, one is not forced to do music at a Low Mass; no law indicates that we must have music all of the time at Mass. Since (knowingly) poorly performed music (and I am speaking here of music that belongs to the choir only – not congregational singing) can never be justified even in extraordinary circumstances, if one is not able to meet the basic standards of Pius X and his reform but instead insists on performing bad music, he is flirting with the grave offence of sacrilege. In order to stay clear of sacrilege, it is simply a matter of knowing the limitations of the choir. Remember that all choirs must consist of properly trained singers. If the choir is not yet able to sing a High Mass, then keep rehearsing for however long it takes to make whatever is performed at the Mass be of the requisite quality. Start modestly, with simple music done well. Keep improving the voices by encouraging continuing vocal training and the perfection of other musical skills. Even if you come from many miles only once a week, strive for the standards that Pius mandated, and only perform the results when you are ready to go before the holy altar of God to give praise and worship, even if it takes weeks or months to prepare the music. By doing this, God will surely be pleased. In addition, remember that poorly performed sacred music can cause frustrating distractions to many members of the congregation, thus impeding their disposition for receiving the graces of the Mass.

dead.[26] We must overcome many obstacles and make many sacrifices in the effort to revive the reform. One should take heart, though, because the task is neither impossible nor even highly improbable. True, it will take time, money, dedication, effort, and determination.[27] Nevertheless, with the help of God, the angels, and the saints, there will be success in establishing the foundation for a revival of the great reform of Pope St. Pius X, and ultimately, a successful restoration of Catholic sacred music.

Pope Saint Pius X,
pray for us!

⧉

---

[26] The fact that rock 'n' roll music has become almost universally prevalent in our society is a stark reminder that we are in grave spiritual trouble. It is abundantly obvious that faith is on the decline, and that vice and evil are dominant today in our society. If one thinks that this is too harsh a criticism of rock music, one should read the history of rock music, where even liberal and highly biased college textbooks will admit the predominant use and/or promotion of drugs, illicit sex, sado-masochism, paganism, violence, and devil worship by all too many rock musicians. It is truly no exaggeration to state that the history of rock music is its own worst indictment.

[27] Here is where the assistance of wealthy individuals and organizations can be of immense help. Great art has most often thrived because wealthy patrons have come forward to help the lives of artists and the fine arts. Now is the time for generous Catholic individuals, businesses, and foundations to help in this great endeavor.

ŚELECT BIBLIOGRAPHY

Amerio, Romano. *Iota Unum. A Study of Changes in the Catholic Church in the XXth century*. Translated from the Second Italian Edition by Fr. John P. Parsons. Kansas City, MO: Sarto House, 1996.

Andrews, H. K. *An Introduction to the Technique of Palestrina*. London: Novello, 1958.

Apel, Willi. *Gregorian Chant*. Bloomington: Indiana University Press, 1958.

——. *The Notation of Polyphonic Music: 900-1600*. 5th edition. Cambridge, MA: The Medieval Academy of America, 1953.

Atlas, Allan W. *Renaissance Music. Music in Western Europe, 1400-1600*. New York: Norton, 1998.

Brill, Patrick J. "Melody in the Motets of T. L. de Victoria and the Palestrina Style. A Comparative Analysis." M.M. Thesis, University of Northern Iowa, 1991.

——. *On Sacred Music: Problems with the Instruction of 1958*. N.p.: Lulu Press, 2009.

Brill, Patrick J. "The Parody Masses of Tomás Luis de Victoria." Ph.D. Dissertation, University of Kansas, 1995.

Brill, Patrick J. "The Tridentine Mass and the Treasury of Catholic Sacred Music." *The Remnant*, July, 1991.

Brown, Howard M. *Music in the Renaissance*. Englewood Cliffs, N.J.: Prentice-Hall, 1976.

Bukofzer, Manfred. *Music in the Baroque Era*. New York: Norton, 1947.

Butcher, S. H., Editor. *Aristotle's Theory of Poetry and Fine Art*. New York: Dover, 1951.

Chiron, Yves. *Annibale Bugnini: Reformer of the Liturgy*. Translated by John Pepino. Brooklyn, NY: Angelico Press, 2018.

Coussemaker, Edmond de. *Histoire de l'harmonie au moyen age*. Paris: V. Didron, 1852.

Davies, Michael. *Pope Paul's New Mass*. Vol III: *Liturgical Revolution*. Dickinson, TX: Angelus Press, 1980.

Hayburn, Robert F. *Papal Legislation on Sacred Music. 95 A.D. to 1977 A.D.* Collegeville, MN: The Liturgical Press, 1979.

Hoppin, Richard H. *Medieval Music.* New York: Norton, 1978.

Jeppesen, Knud. *The Style of Palestrina and the Dissonance.* London, 1927. New York: Dover, 1970.

Kwasniewski, Peter. "Are Women Permitted to Sing the Propers of the Mass?" *New Liturgical Movement*, March 8, 2021.

——. "Coincidences During the Reign of Pius XII? Political Background to Vatican II and Liturgical Changes." *Life-SiteNews*, May 25, 2021.

——. *Good Music, Sacred Music, and Silence: Three Gifts of God for Liturgy and for Life.* Gastonia, NC: TAN Books, 2023.

——. "Lights and Shadows in the Pontificate of Pius XII." *OnePeterFive*, September 22, 2021.

——. "*Sacrosanctum Concilium*: The Ultimate Trojan Horse." *Crisis Magazine*, June 21, 2021.

Meyer, Garrett. "'Other Things Being . . . Equal'? A Critique of *Sacrosanctum Concilium* 116." *New Liturgical Movement*, October 14, 2024.

Paléographie musicale, 17 vols. Solesmes: Abbey Press, 1889–1925.

Reese, Noble, Lockwood, Owens, Kerman, Stevenson. *The New Grove High Renaissance Masters.* New York: Norton, 1980.

Reid, Cornelius L. *The Free Voice: A Guide to Natural Singing.* New York: The Joseph Patelson Music House, 1972.

Romita, Florentius. *Jus musicae liturgicae.* Rome: Edizione Liturgicae, 1947.

Strunk, Oliver. *Source Readings in Music History.* New York: Norton, 1950.

INDEX

ABOUT THE AUTHOR

DR. PATRICK J. BRILL is a commissioned composer who has written numerous classical-style compositions including *a cappella* vocal works, instrumental chamber compositions, symphonic orchestral pieces, and compositions for choir and orchestra.

In 2010, he was commissioned by the Bach Festival Orchestra and Choir of Winter Park to compose Christmas music for the 2011 season. His composition, entitled *Veni, Veni, Emmanuel*, was premiered on December 10 and 11, 2011 as part of the Bach Festival's *A Classic Christmas: Seasonal Music*. It was subsequently performed again in December of 2012 and December of 2013. *Veni, Veni, Emmanuel* was eventually recorded on a CD of Christmas selections with the Bach Festival Choir entitled *All is Bright: A Choral Christmas*.

On August 16, 2024, Dr. Brill's *Royal Coronation Overture*, performed by the Czech Chamber Philharmonic Orchestra Pardubice was released on the Navona Recordings label, distributed by Naxos. Additionally, Dr. Brill's *Scherzo for Orchestra* was recorded recently by the London Symphony Orchestra and will be released on the Navona label in April 2025.

Dr. Brill holds a B. A. in Philosophy from the College (now University) of St. Thomas, and a B. A. in Music from the University of Minnesota, where he studied piano, music history, and music theory/composition. He earned a Master's of Music in music history from the University of Northern Iowa, and holds a Ph.D. in historical musicology from the University of Kansas. As a musicologist, he has published a book on sacred music and authored several musicological articles.

Dr. Brill has taught music history at the University of Kansas, the University of Missouri-Kansas City Music Conservatory, Rockhurst College, Barry University, Columbia College, Troy University, and Eastern Florida State College. He currently teaches music history at Valencia College in Orlando, Florida. Dr. Brill has also taught private piano as well as music theory/composition for many years.

www.ingramcontent.com/pod-product-compliance
Lightning Source LLC
Chambersburg PA
CBHW030304130626
46549CB00002B/680